MONETARY POLICY
The Argument from Keynes' Treatise to Friedman

C. VAN EATON

MONETARY POLICY

The Argument from Keynes' Treatise to Friedman

Edited with Introductions by
WILLIAM HAMOVITCH
QUEENS COLLEGE

D. C. HEATH AND COMPANY · BOSTON

Library of Congress Catalog Card Number: 66-15970

PRINTED JUNE 1966

CONTENTS

v

III. RULES VERSUS DISCRETION: THE FRIEDMAN THESIS

INTRODUCTION

Views on the role of monetary policy in promoting economic stability and growth have undergone considerable shifts in emphasis over the last several decades. In the 1920's, great stock was placed in monetary policy as a stabilizing tool, and it was hailed by some as a major reason for the "new era" prosperity of that period. Among the economists who expressed a positive view of monetary policy as an effective stabilizer was John Maynard Keynes in *Treatise on Money*, published in 1930; the first selection in Part One, which is taken from the *Treatise*, makes this unmistakably clear.

The shattering experience of the Great Depression of the 1930's and the influence of the revolution in economic thought, initiated in large part by Keynes' *The General Theory of Employment, Interest, and Money*, published in 1936, led to disillusionment with many economic institutions and preconceptions. This disillusionment extended to a questioning of the ability of central banks to have a significant effect in controlling economic fluctuations. It is true that, according to the new Keynesian model, monetary authorities could still influence the economy through their control over the supply of money, which — together with the liquidity preference schedule — determines the interest rate. In this model the interest rate, in turn, is one of the key variables determining the volume of investment. One question, however, remains: How sensitive is investment to changes in the interest rate? A number of empirical studies attempting to measure the degree of this sensitivity found it to be very small; and the issue, for many, seemed to be settled. This conclusion is expressed in Part One by H. D. Henderson, a British economist.

The ability of monetary policy to restrict inflation was regarded less pessimistically than its role in stimulating recovery. This view, too, received support from Keynes, according to whom there was a minimum interest rate below which any further increase in the money supply would only go into idle balances. This is the famous liquidity trap, which, at some low rate of interest, assumes a perfectly elastic demand for money and precludes any further drop in the interest rate. When this point is reached, the monetary authorities are powerless to stimulate any rise in expenditures through an increase in the money supply. On the other hand, as there is no theoretical limit to the height of interest rates, there is more possibility of monetary policy being successful in curbing inflation. As a practical matter, however, because of the reluctance of governments to permit excessively high interest rates on the grounds, among others, that this is unduly favorable to creditors and burdensome to debtors, there may be a political, if not an economic, limit. But, if the political objections can be overcome, restrictive monetary policy is potentially effective.

So long as the main concern of economists in the 1930's and well into the 1940's was over depression rather than inflation, attention was diverted from monetary to fiscal policy as the more powerful stabilizing tool. Although economists frequently pointed out that monetary and fiscal policies could and should be used to complement each other in promoting prosperity, in fact monetary policy was relegated to a definitely secondary role in the analysis and discussion of stabilization programs.

From the end of World War II until 1951 the Federal Reserve virtually abandoned its monetary stabilization role. Because of the large public debt resulting from the war, it was believed that a stable orderly market for government bonds was of utmost importance for maintaining confidence in government credit which, in turn, was deemed necessary for sustaining a prosperous economy. It was thought that a rise in interest rates was to be avoided as this would reduce bond prices and thereby impair confidence. The Federal Reserve undertook the task of supporting the government bond market by standing ready to buy any volume of government securities that might be necessary to prevent a decline in their prices. On occasion, this led to its engaging in open-market purchases when monetary ease was not warranted by the state of the economy and so contributed to the post-World War II inflation. Finally, in 1951, with a new burst of inflation emanating from the Korean War, the Federal Reserve and the Treasury reached an accord whereby the former was to be free to influence interest rates while still concerning itself with the problem of promoting an orderly Treasury bond market. The Federal Reserve had now largely, but not completely, recovered its traditional function of monetary control. In the ensuing years, it still has had to consider the Treasury's problems of managing the public debt as one of the factors in monetary policy. The pre-accord period of 1945–51 provides an illustration of what can go wrong when the monetary authorities are given discretionary power; in that period the Federal Reserve followed a policy of government bond support and thereby departed from its economic stabilization role.

Another conflict of goals which has arisen stems from the monetary authorities' concern with a country's balance-of-payments position. For example, if a country has a balance-of-payments deficit, this can be made up by some combination of loss of gold and favorable short-term capital flows (that is, an increase in the inflow of funds from, and a decrease in their outflow to, foreign countries). If it is desired, or even necessary, to limit the loss of gold, one of the most common means to encourage favorable capital flows is to bring about an increase in domestic interest rates. This provides an incentive for foreigners to invest in domestic financial markets and reduces the incentive for investment in foreign markets. If the response to the higher interest rates is sufficiently strong, the result can be a reduction in the gold loss and a restoration of confidence in the country's currency. In addition, high interest rates, by restricting domestic demand, should contribute to prices' being lower than they would otherwise be. If the result is a decrease in domestic, relative to foreign, prices, exports should rise and imports fall, thus reducing or, more hopefully, eliminating the balance-of-payments deficit. The solution may well not be this simple; even if it works, it often poses the problem that such high interest rates may perpetuate or cause a slack in the domestic economy as well as impede long-run growth. The essence of this dilemma is that balance-of-payments considerations may require higher interest rates than are warranted by domestic economic considerations.

In recent years, we have had ample evidence of the aforementioned problem. In late 1964, and continuing into 1965, the British government, through the Bank of England, has embarked on a policy of high interest rates as a means of defending the English pound in the face of a serious balance-of-payments crisis. Concern has been expressed about the possibly adverse effect of this policy on the prosperity and growth of the domestic economy. It is ironic that the restrictive monetary policy should be undertaken at the behest of the newly-elected Labour government, since the Socialists have traditionally opposed high interest rates on the grounds that they help mainly creditors and the wealthy and, at the same time, retard economic growth. The same problem, in less severe form, has also faced the United States in recent years. In the light of balance-of-payments deficits and loss of gold since 1958, the Federal Reserve has, on occasion over the last several years, adopted a somewhat, if only moderately, more stringent monetary policy than would have been the case if no attention were paid to international financial considerations.

Still another conflict can arise among the goals of price stability, full employment and maximum long-run growth. It may well be that the first-mentioned goal calls for periods of slack in the economy which may be effectuated by a restrictive monetary policy and higher interest rates. But this policy prevents a full-employment economy and may also inhibit long-run growth. If, instead, we aim for a high-pressure, full-employment economy, there are inevitable pressures on prices emanating from the forces of high demand. Finally, if maximizing growth through the highest possible level of investment requires maintaining permanently low interest rates, the level of demand may be greater than needed to achieve full employment and, if so, would most certainly exert a strong upward pressure on prices. If this policy were adopted, the goal of price stability would have to be achieved by other tools. The problem is again posed of determining the best combination of goals.

The above discussion and examples of possible conflict of goals do not question the effectiveness of monetary policy. On the contrary, the implication is that it can be very powerful. But what of the argument that it is a weak instrument? As the debate on this issue continued in the post-World War II years, there was a reaction to the low esteem in which monetary policy was held in the 1930's, and some economists undertook a reevaluation of its possible significance as a stabilizing device. This was undoubtedly due in part to the inflation of the period, during which more effectiveness could be expected from monetary policy. Its rejection of earlier years had been, at least in part, based on its presumed weakness in combating depression.

Along with the reappraisal of monetary policy came a shift of emphasis. According to one view, its potential efficacy is due not so much to its effect on the interest rate and, through that, on investment as to its influence on credit availability. According to this approach, when the Federal Reserve tightens credit, the important result is not so much a rise in interest rates as the fact that credit is rationed to the better risks. At the same time, it is argued, other financial intermediaries such as savings banks and insurance companies are restricted in their lending. This is because their holdings of government bonds fall in price with a rise in interest rates, and they are reluctant to accept the capital loss attendant on selling them. Their assets are thus locked in, and they have less potential credit available for borrowers. The preceding argument is presented in these readings by Robert V. Rosa.

In subsequent studies, the validity of the so-called "locking-in" effect has been questioned, as is seen, for example, in the selection by

Warren L. Smith in Part Two. A number of economists, including Smith, contend that the existence of a large public debt and the rise of financial intermediaries have seriously impaired the effectiveness of monetary policy. He argues that when the monetary authorities tighten credit, commercial banks and financial intermediaries can offset this by selling some of their government securities, even at a loss, in order to have funds available for borrowers and thus take advantage of the higher interest returns. This view, which is clearly at variance with Rosa's, does seem to be supported by the weight of evidence so that the attendant conclusion, that the goals of Federal Reserve policies can at least in part be thwarted by the behavior of commercial banks and financial intermediaries, deserves careful attention.

In answer to Smith's argument, it should be noted that if the monetary authorities are willing to pursue a restrictive monetary policy to any limit, they can surely negate the offsetting effects caused by the aforementioned policies of commercial banks and financial intermediaries. This point is made by Joseph Ascheim in a later selection. The question then arises as to whether the degree of monetary restriction has to be so severe as to usher in a recession. But this possible dilemma applies to any stabilization policy with or without the role of financial intermediaries. Can a policy of restraint be devised which is sufficiently strong to prevent excessive expansion and inflation and, at the same time, not so repressive as to cause an economic contraction? The answer to this question is not clear, and it points up once again the possible conflict between the goals of price stability and full employment.

Another criticism of monetary policy is based not on its lack of effectiveness but rather on the thesis that its influence is powerful but frequently perverse, in that it aggravates rather than moderates economic fluctuations. This stems in part from the view that the economy is inherently reasonably stable and that its fluctuations have been due primarily to the instability of credit. According to this assumption, the economy would enjoy maximum stability if money were somehow kept neutral in its effect. Among the policy prescriptions that have followed from this position is the recommendation that there be no control by monetary authorities and that commercial banks be required to keep a reserve of 100 percent against deposits so as to eliminate the destabilizing effects of multiple-credit expansion and contraction. If a monetary authority is created, its powers should be limited by the establishment of fixed rules. This parallels the argument for relying on built-in stabilizers instead of discretionary fiscal policy.

Among the reasons given for opposing discretionary monetary policy is the argument that our ability to forecast general economic activity is not very good and that policies adopted on the basis of the expected combination of accurate and erroneous predictions would cause far more instability than would result if money were allowed to play a passive role. On this point it can be said that, whatever may have been true of the past, our techniques and abilities in this area have been improving so that the chances of incorrect policies based on wrong predictions are reduced although, admittedly, not eliminated. But, it has also been argued, even when a prediction is accurate, monetary policy is often perverse as it affects the economy only after a lengthy lag. This argument will be found in a selection from Milton Friedman's *A Program for Monetary Stability*. In his review of Friedman's book, Abba P. Lerner criticizes Friedman's opposition to discretionary government action and contends that his Rule would permit an excessively high level of unemployment. The final selection, by John Kareken and Robert M. Solow, questions Friedman's estimation of the lag between adoption of a specific policy and its effect.

Another criticism that has been leveled against general monetary policy is that it is discriminatory in its effects. Specifically, it is argued that a tight-money policy falls with particular severity on the small firm because, in contrast to the large established corporations, it does not have access to the same variety of sources of funds. According to this view, the smaller, more competitive firms are hurt relative to the larger, more powerful, and, usually, more monopolistic ones.

Others have argued against the use of high interest rates on the grounds of equity, in that they bring about an unwarranted redistribution of income in favor of the creditors at the expense of the debtors. This conclusion cannot be an unqualified one as must be clear when we realize that some of our biggest and strongest corporations such as American Telephone and Telegraph, and others, are at the same time large debtors.

It should be evident from this introduction that monetary authorities have a most complex task of reconciling a variety of goals. It is in part because of this complexity that some economists favor abandonment of any attempt at discretionary policy. Others, while recognizing the difficulties, argue that we should not surrender to the problems but rather strive to strike a reasoned balance among the various goals. Errors of judgment are undoubtedly made under this approach but it is optimistically concluded that, on the whole, the economy is better served by the use of discretionary policy than by reliance on mechanical rules.

PART ONE

THE EFFECTIVENESS OF MONETARY POLICY: CHANGING VIEWS

JOHN MAYNARD KEYNES

The Control of the Rate of Investment*

In this selection Keynes expresses the view that central banks are able to exert a strong influence on investment and thereby maintain stability of income and prices. He recognizes the difficulty of reversing a condition of economic instability once it has been allowed to develop and suggests that considerable time may be required to reverse it. He also touches on the difficulties which can develop from adherence to an international standard. These are the problems arising from a conflict in the goals of domestic economic stability and balance-of-payments equilibrium which were discussed in the Introduction of this book. But granted these and other difficulties, Keynes defends the proposition that central banks are able to maintain an equilibrium level of investment and savings and, through that, a stable economy, by keeping the market rate equal to the natural rate of interest, which the Treatise defines as the rate that equilibrates savings and investment. He argues that the existence of credit cycles and

* Abridged from A Treatise on Money, Volume II, by John Maynard Keynes, pp. 339–387. Reprinted by permission of Harcourt, Brace & World, Inc., Macmillan & Co., Ltd., and the Trustees of the Estate of the late Lord Keynes.

1

economic instability in the past was due to the divergence of the market and natural rates of interest and that this divergence can be prevented by farsighted and bold central bank action. It is interesting to note in the latter part of the selection that Keynes, writing in 1930 after the Great Depression had started, still expressed high hopes that if the monetary authorities succeeded in driving interest rates down to a very low level, investment could well be stimulated sufficiently to stabilize prices and bring the contraction to an end. Keynes, of course, subsequently changed his approach to stabilization policy and, six years later in *The General Theory*, developed a model which contributed to an emphasis on fiscal policy and a relative downgrading of monetary policy. We do find a hint of doubt in this selection, but essentially it maintains a note of confidence in the stabilization powers of monetary policy.

CAN THE BANKING SYSTEM CONTROL
THE PRICE-LEVEL?

I REACH at last the crux of the whole matter. We have endeavoured to analyse and to classify the multifarious factors which determine the price-level and the means by which the Central Bank in a Closed System, or the aggregate behavior of Central Banks throughout the world, can influence and dominate the behavior of the banking and monetary system as a whole. But when all is said and done, does it lie within the power of a Central Bank in actual practice to pursue a policy which will have the effect of fixing the value of money at any prescribed level? If, for example, the duty of preserving the stability of the purchasing power of money within narrow limits were to be laid upon a Central Bank by law, would it be possible for the Central Bank to fulfill this obligation in all circumstances?

Those who attribute sovereign power to the monetary authority in the governance of prices do not, of course, claim that the terms on which money is supplied is the *only* influence affecting the price-level. To maintain that the supplies in a reservoir can be maintained at any required level by pouring enough water into it, is not inconsistent with admitting that the level of the reservoir depends on many other factors besides how much water is poured in, — for example, the natural rainfall, evaporation, leakage and the habits of the users of the system. Such a claim would only be unjustified if the amount of evaporation or leakage or other source of loss, or the consumption of those using the system, were a direct function of the amount of water poured in, of such a character that the more poured in the greater for that reason the consumption or the diminution in the natural rainfall or other occasion of loss, so that no amount of inflow would raise the supplies in the reservoir above a certain level. Which of these alternatives is the true analogy for the effect on the price-level of the creation of additional supplies of money by the banking system?

I have more sympathy today than I had a few years ago with some of the doubts and hesitations such as were expressed in 1927 by Governor Strong and other witnesses before the Committee of the United States Congress on Stabilization. This Committee was appointed to examine the wisdom of a proposed amendment to the Federal Reserve Act, the effect of which would have been to lay upon the Federal Reserve Board the duty of using all the powers at its disposal to "promote a stable price-level for commodities in general." The reasonable doubts of practical men, towards the idea that "the Federal Reserve System has the power to raise or lower the price-level by some automatic method, by some magic mathematical formula,"[1] are well expressed in the following extracts:

GOVERNOR STRONG.[2] I believe there is a tendency to look at the price-level as though it operated up and down against a counter-weight of credit, and as if you could open a spigot when prices are declining and put a little more credit in the counter-weight and raise prices, and if prices are going up you could drain a little credit out of the counter-weight and let prices go down. But I am afraid the price problem is much more complicated than that.

I would like to describe to you a situation which is very recent, to show how the relation of a price movement to other elements that we take into consideration presents a real practical puzzle of management. Two months ago there was some concern felt in the country as to the extent of speculation in stocks and the amount of credit which was being employed in support of that speculation. At the same time, our studies of the price structure showed very clearly that there was taking place, and had for some little time taken place, a decline in the wholesale price-level, and when we came to analyse that decline we found that it was

[1] Governor Strong before the Stabilization Committee, p. 295.
[2] I have pieced the following into a continuous narrative from scattered passages in Governor Strong's evidence before the Stabilization Committee — pp. 295, 359, 550, 577.

almost entirely due to a decline in the prices of cotton and grains. Assume that we here are the directors of the Federal Reserve Bank trying to determine what to do about the discount rate. We have this feeling that there is a growth of speculation; possibly a feeling that it ought to be curbed by the Federal Reserve System in some way. On the other hand, we are faced with a clear indication of some decline in the price of farm commodities. Now, if very great concern had been felt about the price of farm commodities, and we felt that the introduction of credit into the market or lowering interest rate might correct the prices of those individual commodities, what might the consequences be in speculation? There you are between the devil and the deep sea.

I believe that administration of credit such as is afforded by the Federal Reserve System is capable of exerting an influence upon the volume of credit employed by the country and upon the cost of that credit. Within the limitations which the volume and the cost of credit exert an influence upon the price-level, and only within that limitation, can the operations of the Federal Reserve System influence prices. But there will be times when even the power to somewhat regulate the volume of credit and its cost will fail of complete or anything like complete regulation of the price-level, because there are many other things, far beyond the influence of the volume and cost of credit, such as the mood of the people. Therefore, if any expression is contained in the Federal Reserve Act which appears to represent to the people that the Federal Reserve System can do more in stabilizing the price-level than the limited control of credit is capable of performing, I am afraid that disappointment will come when there are fluctuations of prices which cannot be controlled within the strict limitations I have described.

When the Federal Reserve System has an adequate volume of earning assets, it has a very considerable capacity to control a runaway movement of prices. But when you get to a decline in prices, one of those insidious periods of liquidation, and not a sharp movement like in 1921 — one of these very difficult slow price movements, possibly not attributable to credit operations at all — what is the Federal Reserve System to do? There is a present decline of prices. Possibly the spirit of optimism of last year has resulted in all merchants contracting for goods which they expected to sell, but are unable to sell when delivered; in other words, there is an overstock of goods beyond what the trade will consume or the people will consume. If there is a margin of goods for sale beyond the capacity of consumption, the introduction of more credit into the credit system will not correct that until the goods are consumed, and that situation arises in the form of contracts long before it can be detected in any reports on volume of business, inventories, or anything of that sort. The amount of goods being transported over the railroads will be just the same; the amount of employment will be just the same. Everything will be marching along with all outward evidence of a sound business situation, but when the public, for one or another reason, slows down in buying and consuming goods, which starts a declining price movement, I don't see how we can correct it.

If we had such a severe decline in the value of cotton and all the commodities that are influenced by world market prices as to cause a decline in the general price-level, and we should attempt to remedy it just by buying securities and making cheap money, it would not cause an advance, certainly not immediately, in the prices of those commodities whose prices are fixed by world markets and world competition. It would have an inflationary effect which might indeed affect price-levels of purely domestic commodities; and if it did, it would be thereby advancing the price of everything the farmer consumed, at the same time that the selling price for what he produces was being reduced.

Take the situation at the present time and for quite a period past. We have had a remarkably stable level of prices for general commodities, with the exception in the last few months of a decline in grain and cotton prices. Prices of cattle and hogs have remained pretty steady. There has been a decline in agricultural prices sufficient to bring about a gradual reduction in the index number of general prices. Now, take the problem of today. Is the Federal Reserve System to step in and attempt to regulate this movement which seems to have started; and if so, how? That is the practical thing that the price regulator would face from time to time.

MR. WILLIAMSON. Do you think that the Federal Reserve Board could, as a matter of fact, stabilize price-levels to a greater extent than they have in the past, by giving greater expansion to market operations and restriction or extension of credit facilities?

GOVERNOR STRONG. I personally think that the administration of the Federal Reserve System since the reaction of 1921 has been just as nearly directed as reasonable human wisdom could direct it toward that very object.

Then there is another possibility that has always struck me as inherent in any recognition of a power resting anywhere to regulate prices, and that is in the everlasting contest that takes place with all humanity between the producer and the consumer. . . . It seems to me that if the Federal Reserve System is recognized as a price regulator, it is going to be somewhat in the position of the poor man who tried to stop a row between an Irishman and his wife. They both turned in and beat him.

MR. WINGO. And you are afraid that without giving you any power that you do not already possess, or without making it possible for you to have any greater desire or ability to serve the common good, the country will be led to believe that by mere legislative declaration the capacity to remove all the economic evils incident to fluctuations of credit will be lodged in this super-wise Board.

GOVERNOR STRONG. Thank you, Mr. Wingo. You express it better than I could.

The following from Dr. Stewart's evidence on the same occasion is also instructive:

DR. WALTER STEWART.[3] Let us assume that there is a recession of building activity, that this carries with it some unemployment in the production of automobiles; let us further assume that the crops turn out sufficiently large to enable us to make large exports, but because of certain disturbances in Europe and the lack of foreign confidence in investments there develops a sagging tendency in the general level of commodity prices. What is there that the Federal Reserve System can do? Suppose, for instance, these prices move off 5 per cent. As I understand it, those who favour the proposal before the Committee believe that by a change of the discount rate, or by open market operations, the international price-level will be given stability. We are not talking about the price-level in the United States, for when we speak of the gold price-level we are talking about the international price-level. I believe that in such a situation an increase or decrease of a small percentage in the discount rates will have little bearing on the price situation.

To what extent, by an addition to credits at a time when prices are declining, not as an aftermath of war inflation but of maladjustments in business, can you cure the causes which lie back of declining prices? My point is that in such circumstances you take a chance of aggravating the very causes which are responsible for the declining prices. If stocks are accumulating and the mood of the community is speculative, then an attempt to use credit for the purpose of stabilizing prices is more likely to aggravate the causes responsible for the movement in prices.

To assume that declining prices, which are after all largely a readjustment to take care of the mistakes made previously, can be overcome by an additional extension of credit is more likely to add to the difficulties in the situation rather than to cure it.

Ease in the money market will be reflected in the demand for certain investment securities, and possibly in a bidding up of speculative securities. But we have had in this country periods when money has remained very easy for more than a year, as in 1908, and yet business remained depressed, not because money was not available at easy rates, but because business was going through a readjustment. Business will continue to go through such readjustments as long as human judgment has to be used and mistakes are made, and to say you can save business from the risks it necessarily assumes by a credit policy which is exercised by the Reserve Banks is an unwarranted assumption.

I think we meet periods in which credit is inflated in the sense of being extended beyond the capacity of industry to use it for productive purposes, even on a declining price-level.

These are reasonable doubts expressed by persons of great experience. They cannot be dispelled merely by pointing to the truism

[3] Pieced together from passages *op. cit.* — pp. 769–775.

of a Quantity Equation. In a sense they can only be dispelled by the prolonged success of an actual attempt at scientific control. But I should like to try to show that the prospects of such an attempt are sufficiently promising for it to be worth a trial.

We have claimed to prove in this Treatise that the price-level of output depends on the level of money-incomes relatively to efficiency, on the volume of investment (measured in cost of production) relatively to saving, and on the "bearish" or "bullish" sentiment of capitalists relatively to the supply of savings-deposits available in the banking system. We have claimed, further, that the banking system can control the supply of savings-deposits, and hence the third factor; that it can by the terms of credit influence to any required extent the volume of investment, and hence the second factor; and that the indirect effects of its influence on the value and the volume of investment determine the money offers which entrepreneurs make to the factors of production, and hence the third factor. But we have *not* claimed that the banking system can produce any of these effects instantaneously; or that it can be expected always to foresee the operation of non-monetary factors in time to take measures in advance to counteract their influence on prices; or that it can avoid violent fluctuations in the prices of different classes of commodities relatively to one another; or that a Central Bank, which is a member of an international system, can preserve domestic stability irrespective of the behavior of other Central Banks.

Some of the occasions of doubt expressed by Governor Strong and Dr. Stewart are conceded by these qualifications. Dr. Stewart's evidence, in particular, emphasized the interdependence of American prices and world prices. But putting aside for the moment the question of international complications, to which we will return in a later section of this chapter, how far are we prepared to attribute to a Central Bank a greater degree of influence on the price-level than these authorities believed it to have?

I think that in one fundamental respect they have mistaken the character of the problem and have under-estimated the possibilities of control. For they have not perceived the vital difference between the production of consumption-goods and the production of investment-goods, and have not allowed, in consequence, for the effect of an increased production of investment-goods on the state of demand for, and hence the price-level of, consumption-goods.

This is partly the result, perhaps, of the traditional view which the banking system has always taken of its own functions. In actual fact the banking system has a dual function — the direction of the supply of resources for working capital through the loans which it makes to producers to cover their outgoings during the period of production (and no longer), and of the supply *pari passu* of the current cash required for use in the Industrial Circulation; and, on the other hand, the direction of the supply of resources which determines the value of securities through the investments which it purchases directly and the loans which it makes to the Stock Exchange and to other persons who are prepared to carry securities with borrowed bank-money, and of the supply *pari passu* of the savings-deposits required for use in the Financial Circulation to satisfy the bullishness or bearishness of financial sentiment, so as to prevent its reacting on the value and the volume of new investment. The statistical proportion of a bank's financial activities to its industrial activities varies widely, but, in the modern world, it will seldom be less than one-half, and may sometimes rise to equality. Yet there is a notion kept up amongst respectable bankers (I am speaking of London—perhaps this is not true of New York) that the first function is the *proper* function of banking, that its needs must always have the first claim on their resources, and that the second function (particularly in so far as it relates to loans for the purpose of carrying securities or other fixed assets) is something to be apologetic about, the importance of which is to be minimized, something which the bankers would like to avoid altogether if they could. The reasons given for this are that the second category of business, namely the financial business, is not self-liquidating and savors of "speculation."

Yet it is doubtful whether these reasons are as valid as they seem. Any given financial loan is probably more liquid than any given industrial loan, and financial loans, which are seldom made except on good security, probably lead to fewer bad debts than industrial loans; whilst the whole body of financial loans and the whole body of industrial loans are equally non-liquid in the sense that no material reduction in the aggregate of either can be made quickly without disaster, the former — if there is anything to choose between them — being probably the easier to curtail of the two, since the assets will be taken over at a price by the holders of savings-deposits. As for "speculation," it is probably true that the banks have to be more on the look-out against ill-informed and reckless borrowers in the case of financial loans than in the case of industrial loans. But, apart from this, the supply of increased credit for providing working capital ought sometimes to be encouraged and sometimes to be discouraged, just as much as the supply of increased credit for carrying fixed capital; and in both cases the pressure of borrowers is likely to be greatest at times when it is least desirable to satisfy it in full, and smallest at times when it is most to be encouraged.

At any rate, when we are considering the *regulative* powers and functions of the banking system, we must study its influence over the rate of investment in fixed capital at least as much as its influence over the rate of investment in working capital; indeed it is probably true that it cannot, in most cases, exert an effective influence over the latter except through its influence over the former. Therefore we shall not understand the full measure of control which the banking system is capable of exerting on the price-level unless we take account of all the ways in which it can influence the rate of investment as a whole.

A further quotation from Dr. Stewart's evidence before the U.S. Stabilization Committee[4] may help to elucidate my point:

There seems to be in this proposal the suggestion that the aim of Federal Reserve policy should be to stabilize the general level of commodity prices. I would be inclined to state the aim and responsibility of the Federal Reserve System somewhat differently. I would say that the responsibility that rests upon Central Banks abroad and the Federal Reserve System in this country is primarily one of maintenance of sound credit conditions. I realize that the term "sound credit conditions" is a vague one. What is meant depends on what one regards sound functions of credit to be. The function of commercial uses of credit is simply to facilitate the production and the marketing of commodities with the maintenance of adequate stocks of commodities in order that the marketing may be orderly. . . . I can see a situation where prices may be declining, yet inventories of commodities were accumulating, and where, if additional credit were granted, it would be used for the purpose of adding to the stock and would mean simply encouraging the accumulation of additional stocks . . . so that, rather than use the price index as a test, I would prefer to know what the inventories were and whether or not production was moving promptly into distribution.

. . . I should not expect the cheapness and abundance of credit to have much effect, by itself, in over-encouraging the market to carry redundant stocks. The market is never eager to carry redundant stocks, and the degree of its willingness to do so chiefly depends on its expectations of the future course of prices. At the best the existence of such stocks will keep prices below the normal cost of production of the commodities concerned and will act as an effective drag on the volume of current output.

But, in any case, this definition of "sound credit conditions" is, to my way of thinking, too narrow. It does not allow for the fact that,

[4] *Op. cit.* p. 763.

if the inability to sell current output at the current cost of production is *general* and not confined to a few special commodities, this is an indication of a maladjustment on the side of *demand* rather than of supply, that the only way of influencing demand is by increasing investment relatively to saving, and that this ought to lead the thoughts of the controllers of the banking system away from the "commercial uses of credit" to its financial uses. To refrain from lowering the rate of interest during a slump for fear of increasing the accumulation of stocks could only have the effect of accentuating the violence of the Credit Cycle; though — I should admit — in conceivable circumstances and as compared with conceivable alternatives, of perhaps shortening its duration.

According to my own definition "sound credit conditions" would, of course, be those in which the market-rate of interest was equal to the natural-rate, and both the value and the cost of new investment were equal to the volume of current savings. If we take this as our criterion, many of Governor Strong's perplexities will become much less formidable. We could, I think, in each case tell him — in general terms — what he ought to do to preserve the stability of the general price-level.

Granted, however, that the Banking System can control the price-level if it can control the value and volume of current investment, certain limitations which we have not yet removed are suggested by doubts whether in practice it does always lie within the power of the Banking System to control the rate of investment. To this question we will now address ourselves. But it may be convenient that I should summarize forthwith my final conclusions as to the limitations, which must be ultimately conceded, on the actual power of the Banking System to control the price-level:

(*a*) It is much easier to preserve stability than to restore it quickly, after a serious state of disequilibrium has been allowed to set in. Thus, if we are asked to start control operations in a situation which is already unstable, we may find that the position has got, for the time being, beyond effective control.

(*b*) Granted all reasonable intelligence and foresight on the part of the managers of the monetary system, non-monetary causes of instability may sometimes arise so suddenly that it is impossible to counteract them in time. In this event it may be inevitable that an interval should elapse before stability can be restored.

(*c*) If there are strong social or political forces causing spontaneous changes in the money-rates of efficiency-wages, the control of the price-level may pass beyond the power of the banking system.

The effective power of the latter is primarily to prevent forces from operating which tend towards induced changes. It can, of course, provoke induced changes to balance spontaneous changes; but it may not be able, in that case, to control the pace or the route of the journey towards the new position of equilibrium.

(*d*) If a country adheres to an international standard and that standard is itself unstable, it is, of course, impossible to preserve the stability of the domestic price-level in face of this. But even if the international standard is itself stable, it may still be impossible to keep the domestic price-level stable if the changes in the demand schedule for capital in terms of the rate of interest are different at home from what they are abroad.

(*e*) Even where the banking system is strong enough to preserve the *stability* of the price-level, it does not follow that it is strong enough both to *alter* the price-level and to establish equilibrium at the new level without long delays and frictions.

In short, I should attribute to the banking system much greater power to *preserve* investment equilibrium than to force the prevailing rate of money-incomes away from the existing level or from the level produced by spontaneous changes, to a new and changed level imposed by conditions abroad or by arbitrary decree at home.

It follows that our existing currency system, in which we frequently impose on our Central Banks the duty of altering their domestic price-levels and rates of money-incomes as the necessary condition of maintaining the convertibility of their domestic currencies in terms of the international standard, puts on them a much more onerous and technically difficult task than that which would confront a Supernational Currency Authority charged with the duty of maintaining stability and armed with full powers and the firm confidence of its constituents. . . .

CAN THE BANKING SYSTEM CONTROL THE RATE OF INVESTMENT?

We have not, as yet, made more than a very little progress towards answering this question in the affirmative. We have shown that the long-term market-rate of interest can be influenced to a certain extent in the desired direction by movements of the short-term rate. But even if the market-rate changes a little, the natural-rate may be changing much faster. For our conclusion to hold, it is necessary, therefore, that we should raise a presumption of an ability on the part of the Banking System to cause the market-rate of interest to move as much and as quickly as the natural-rate is likely to move in any ordinary circumstances.

We shall not be able to prove this by an appeal to statistics. For the mere occurrence of a Credit Cycle is in itself a demonstration of the fact that the Banking System has failed to change the market-rate so as to keep pace with changes in the natural-rate. It is certain, therefore, that hitherto the Banking System has not succeeded in controlling the Rate of Investment with sufficient success to avoid serious instability.

Thus we cannot do more at present than marshal the various means at the disposal of the Banking System. Only the future can show for certain whether the conscious and well-directed use of all these means, confidently employed in the right degree and at the right time, is capable of solving the problem.

THE SLUMP OF 1930

I am writing these concluding lines in the midst of the world-wide slump of 1930. The wholesale Indexes have fallen by 20 per cent in a year. The prices of a large group of the world's most important staple commodities — wheat, oats, barley, sugar, coffee; cotton, wool, jute, silk; copper, tin, spelter; rubber — stood a year ago 50 per cent higher in price than they do now. The American Index of Production has receded by more than 20 per cent. In Great Britain, Germany and the United States at least 10,000,000 workers stand unemployed. One cannot but be moved by a feeling of the importance of diagnosing correctly the scientific causes of these misfortunes. Was the catastrophe avoidable? Can it be remedied? . . .

The remedy should come, I suggest, from a general recognition that the rate of investment need not be beyond our control, if we are prepared to use our banking systems to effect a proper adjustment of the market-rate of interest. It might be sufficient merely to produce a general belief in the long continuance of a very low rate of short-term interest. The change, once it has begun, will feed on itself.

Of specific remedies the argument of this chapter suggests two as appropriate to the occasion. The Bank of England and the Federal Reserve Board might put pressure on their member banks to do what would be to the private advantage of these banks if they were all to act together, namely, to reduce the rate of interest which they allow to depositors to a very low figure, say ½ per cent. At the same time these two central institutions should pursue bank-rate policy and

open-market operations *à outrance,* having first agreed amongst themselves that they will take steps to prevent difficulties due to international gold movements from interfering with this. That is to say,
they should combine to maintain a very low level of the short-term
rate of interest, and buy long-dated securities either against an expansion of Central Bank money or against the sale of short-dated securities until the short-term market is saturated. It happens that this is an
occasion when, if I am right, one of the conditions limiting open-
market operations *à outrance* does not exist; for it is not an occasion
— at least not yet — when bonds are standing at a price above reasonable expectations as to their long-term normal, so that they can still
be purchased without the prospect of a loss.

Not until deliberate and vigorous action has been taken along
such lines as these and has failed, need we, in the light of the argument of this Treatise, admit that the Banking System can *not,* on
this occasion, control the rate of investment and, therefore, the level
of prices.

H. D. HENDERSON

The Significance of the Rate of Interest*

Henderson supports the view held by many economists in the 1930's
and '40's that changes in interest rates are not very important in
affecting the volume of investment. The author argues that inventory
investment depends upon needs as reflected in the volume of sales
and is likely to be little influenced by changes in the interest rate. For
investment in machinery, he suggests that there is so much uncertainty
with regard to the obsolescence and profitability factors that interest
rates appear insignificant by comparison. He does grant that investment in long-lived assets like buildings and public utilities may be

* From H. D. Henderson, "The Significance of the Rate of Interest," Oxford
Economic Papers, No. 1 (1938), pp. 16–27. Reprinted by permission of the
Clarendon Press, Oxford.

substantially affected by changes in the interest rate. He minimizes even this potential role, however, by the argument that the volume of government public works and private utility investment is likely to be affected more by countercyclical considerations than by interest rate changes and that the volume of residential construction will be low because of a probable decline in population growth and hence in new families. Neither of these arguments is very convincing. While a portion of government spending on public works might be expected to be affected primarily by cyclical considerations, the same cannot be said for all public-works spending and certainly not for privately-owned utilities. On the other question, the population curve happened to move upward after World War II and residential construction has in fact been an important part of total investment.

Henderson also suggests that changes in interest rate may affect the economy through the effect on bond and stock prices which generally rise in response to low, and fall in response to high, interest rates. According to the author, if interest rates are reduced and bond and stock prices consequently rise, consumers will increase their spending, especially for luxury goods, as they make capital gains or, at least, paper profits. He adheres, though, to his fundamental conclusion on the relative unimportance of interest rate changes and for support alludes to empirical studies undertaken by a group of Oxford economists. According to these studies, based on interviews of leading British businessmen, interest rate changes played little or no role in investment decisions. Subsequently, similar studies were made in the United States with the same conclusion. Many economists were led to downgrade monetary policy as an effective means of offsetting economic fluctuations because of these studies and the type of reasoning advanced by Henderson. It should be noted, however, that although Henderson minimizes the effectiveness of changes in the interest rate, he does not completely dismiss its role.

Few economic questions are of greater interest and importance today than that of the part played by the rate of interest in the working of the economic system, and the influence exerted by changes in interest rates on trade activity. The maintenance of cheap money has been a central feature of the economic policy pursued by the

British Government since 1932; and this has undoubtedly been largely responsible for the marked reduction in the general level of interest rates that has followed. The fall in interest rates has made the government's financial task of balancing the budget materially easier. There is thus a natural and strong predisposition in official circles to believe in the importance of low interest rates and to claim that the lower rates established have been a material factor in promoting general economic recovery.

For different reasons this predisposition is shared by the majority of academic economists. Withdrawn, as he is, from close contact with the details of the economic system, the academic economist is especially interested in those forces which are at work throughout the economic system as a whole, and the importance of which appears to be fundamental. The rate of interest is a force of this character. The movement in gilt-edged interest rates from the level of 4½ per cent or more which prevailed until 1932 to the level of 3 per cent or less which was established in 1935 is to the detached student of economic affairs an event of great interest and intrinsic dignity, and his mind is ready to welcome the idea that it may have played an immensely important part in ways not easy perhaps to detect in detail, in the changes that have taken place in economic activity. This inclination is strengthened by the widespread preoccupation of economic analysis in recent years with the relations between savings and investment. While economists have been divided by abstract and complex issues as to the relative importance of the forces by which the rate of interest is determined, there has been little dispute as to the importance of its consequences. That a large part of the prolonged economic malaise of the post-war period might be attributable to a rate of interest markedly in excess of the level required for equilibrium is a doctrine agreeable to the instincts of economists of both orthodox and heretical leanings.

Thus both official circles and academic economists have a bias in favor of propagating the view that lower interest rates have been a major factor in recovery. Nor is the business community predisposed to quarrel with it. To the industrialist or trader, who works with borrowed money, lower interest rates mean a reduction in his costs. The reduction may not strike him as particularly important; nonetheless he welcomes it. Banks, insurance companies, and others who lend money for interest may be adversely affected, it is true, by lower interest rates, so far as their annual income is concerned; but owing to the consequential rise in security values many of them derive a compensatory benefit in the shape of a stronger balance-sheet position. Thus, up to a point at least, most lenders are not inclined to cavil at cheaper money. The investing public also welcomes the rise in security values. Low interest rates, in short, either are or seem to be to the material advantage of the great majority of the economic community. Add to this the natural tendency of the human mind to accept *post hoc* as *propter hoc,* and it is not surprising that the idea that cheap money has been one of the chief factors in economic recovery should have been accepted by public opinion in general as an established, if somewhat mysterious, truth.

Yet beneath this impressive harmony of outward acceptance there lurks a widespread bewilderment and detailed scepticism. If the question is put "What is the *modus operandi* by which low interest rates stimulate economic activity?" there are few who are ready to offer a coherent answer, and they include hardly any one who is intimately acquainted with the actual working of the economic system. Consider some of the difficulties that arise. Are lower interest rates really effective in inducing businessmen to undertake operations that they would not otherwise have undertaken? If so, what sort of businessmen and what sort of operations? Will manufacturers or traders be induced to purchase additional stocks of materials? There are obvious difficulties in supposing an affirmative answer to these questions. By increasing his stocks in excess of his requirements the manufacturer or trader will incur an unnecessary expense. Lower interest rates, it is true, will make this expense less than it would otherwise have been. But there will be an avoidable expense, and the question arises why either the manufacturer or trader should deliberately incur it. He may, of course, calculate that the prices of his materials are likely to rise or that the demand for his products will increase. If so, it is this expectation of higher prices or increased sales rather than the cheaper terms of borrowing that will constitute the real inducement. Moreover, in this event it is difficult to suppose that variations in interest rates will be an important factor in the calculation. No one is ever able to estimate with precision the magnitude and degree of probability attaching to an expected rise of prices. A man may form an opinion that it is more likely than not that prices will rise by anything from 5 to 10 per cent or more in the next few months. His opinion will seldom be more precise than that. If, on such grounds, he decides that it is wise to purchase now in excess of his normal requirements, one would expect him to come to the same conclusion even if the annual charges for a bank overdraft were 1 or 2 per cent higher than they are.

It may be, of course, that changes in interest rates constitute one of the reasons why businessmen expect prices to rise or trade to improve. There is little doubt, indeed, that this is true in some degree; for there is a fairly well-recognized tradition that a low bank rate helps to promote a rise of prices and greater trade activity. A rise in bank rate to a really high figure would undoubtedly be regarded by many businessmen as a warning signal enjoining a policy of caution, and, conversely, reductions in bank rate of a low figure probably serve as an influence inducing businessmen in a strong financial position to regard the business outlook more hopefully. It is clear enough, therefore, that changes in bank rate may, and probably do, exert some influence on business activity through the channel of psychology. But two observations suggest themselves. First, it hardly seems reasonable to suppose that this influence can be of major importance. There have been times when bank rate has remained low for a long period before any recovery in commodity prices has ensued. Most businessmen are concerned, moreover, not with the general movement of prices but with the prices of certain particular commodities which they buy or sell. It is difficult to suppose that they could give a very prominent place to reductions of bank rate in forming their view of the prospects of the markets in which they are interested. Secondly, whatever may be the practical importance of this influence, it leaves the essential question unanswered. Presumably the expectation that lower bank rate will make for better trade or higher prices rests on some rational foundation; otherwise its influence would be precarious. What, then, is the solid basis for this expectation? The essential link in the chain of cause and effect has still to be discovered.

Let us pass then to another possibility. Is it reasonable to suppose that lower interest rates may stimulate long-term capital expenditure by businessmen, that manufacturers, for example, may be encouraged to extend their works or introduce new and improved machinery? At first sight an affirmative answer to this question seems more plausible; but when it is closely examined rather similar difficulties arise. We may suppose a manufacturer to be considering the question as to whether he should install some new labor-saving machine which will entail a certain saving in his wages bill for a given volume of output. The annual saving thus effected may be estimated with some precision. There is no difficulty in supposing that it may be computed so as to represent some definite percentage of the capital cost of the machine. If the machine could be expected to last for ever or for a long period, such as 20 or 30 years, there would also be no difficulty in supposing that a difference of 1 or 2 per cent in the long-term rate of interest might turn the scales of the calculation as to whether it was worth while to introduce the machine. In fact, however, most modern labor-saving machinery has a comparatively brief period of effective life. The same progress of invention which has given rise to the machine which the manufacturer is considering may, a few years later, produce a still better machine which will effect still larger reductions in the annual wages bill. In calculating, therefore, the profitability of introducing the machine a rapid rate of obsolescence must be assumed. In other words, the machine must be expected to pay for itself over a comparatively few years; not 20 or 30 years, but 7 or perhaps 5 or perhaps 3. This, however, makes it much harder to translate the problem into terms of a calculation of annual gain and loss in which the rate of interest is likely to be a material factor. For if such a calculation is made, the allowance for obsolescence or depreciation will inevitably be a much larger item on the debit side than the charge for interest. Yet the allowance for obsolescence must necessarily be of an arbitrary rough-and-ready character, and the event may diverge from it materially in the one direction or the other. The machine which is assumed to have an effective life of 5 years may actually be retained for 7 or, on the other hand, it may become obsolete in 3. Thus a high degree of uncertainty would necessarily attach to any calculation of annual gain or loss, and it is hard to suppose that a difference in interest rates, which could only represent a small item in the calculation, could play a material part in the decision reached. It is doubtful, indeed, whether many manufacturers calculate the profitability of a new machine along lines which take account of variations in the rate of interest.

A large part of a manufacturer's fixed capital may not, of course, be of a highly obsolescent character. It will represent rather buildings and fixed equipment which will usually have a long period of effective life. But if it is easier in this case to calculate with precision the annual cost represented by the capital, it is much more difficult to calculate with precision the annual return which it is likely to yield. If a manufacturer is considering whether to put up new works which will enlarge his productive capacity, his dominating question, it is natural to suppose, will be whether he is likely to be able to sell profitably the extra output of goods. This is a question which seldom lends itself to precise calculation, and it is again hard, therefore, on general grounds, to suppose that many manufacturers would pay much attention to the prevailing rate of interest in deciding to enlarge their productive capacity. There remains the possibility that a manufacturer may choose a period of low interest rates to execute capital extensions which he has decided on other grounds to undertake before very long. But here again an awkward question suggests itself. Is this consideration likely to weigh for very much in practice as compared, for example, with the level of building costs?

There are, then, serious difficulties in supposing that a change in interest rates will exert any very important influence of a direct character on the capital expenditure of the ordinary trader or manufacturer, whether upon working capital or fixed capital. There remain other classes of capital goods, in respect of which these difficulties are less formidable. There are those capital goods the demand for which comes not from manufacturers or traders, but from private individuals, i.e. durable consumers' goods, the leading instance of which is a house or other dwelling. It is comparatively easy to see how a change in the rate of interest may affect materially the demand for houses. The utility of a house to its occupier does not depend, as a rule, on any uncertainty as to the profits he can make from living in it; he can therefore estimate directly the annual value to him of a house of a certain size and quality in a particular place. On the other hand, a house lasts for a long period of years and the interest on its capital cost is not, therefore, unimportant as compared with the allowance that must be made for its depreciation. There is no difficulty, therefore, in supposing that a substantial fall in the rate of interest may give a material stimulus to house building.

There are also durable capital goods which are owned neither by manufacturers, traders, nor private consumers but by public authorities, such as the state or municipalities. Capital goods of this character comprise a vast variety of types, and they account in the aggregate for a large proportion of the accumulated capital of the community. Here, as in the case of houses, the normal life of the capital goods is so long as to make the rate of interest a major factor in computing the annual cost. Their utility may be of a type which it is hard to measure in financial terms at all; but in such cases it is usually independent of necessarily doubtful calculations as to future earning capacity. On the other hand, where the capital goods are of a commercial character and represent the capital equipment of trading services such as gas or electricity, it is usually possible to calculate the probable demand for their services with a fair degree of precision. This last consideration applies also to public utility concerns. It is therefore possible that such concerns in considering whether to modernize their plant or enlarge their capacity might measure the expected annual yield against the cost of the capital expenditure in a way that would take account of the prevailing rate of interest. There is thus no fundamental difficulty in supposing that changes in the rate of interest may exert a considerable effect on the amount of capital expenditure undertaken by public authorities and public utility concerns.

The broad effect of the foregoing argument is to suggest that the influence of the rate of interest on capital expenditure is far less general and all-pervasive in character than is commonly assumed in economic discussion. There are only two types of capital goods on which it is plausible to suppose that expenditure might be appreciably stimulated by a lower, or appreciably retarded by a higher, rate of interest, namely (1) durable consumers' goods, and (2) the assets of public bodies and public utilities. These two classes of capital goods are both of very great importance; and over a period of years it is probable that they account between them for a very high proportion of our aggregate capital expenditure. If, therefore, the influence of the rate of interest were limited to these two spheres it might be a factor of great consequence; but it would be less automatic and reliable than is sometimes assumed. So far as the second category is concerned, the decision whether or not to undertake public works expenditure of a non-commercial character will seldom, if ever, be determined solely on financial grounds. Many considerations of policy, both local and national, will be taken into account. There is nowadays, for example, a growing advocacy of the view that public bodies and public utilities should regulate their capital expenditure systematically with the object of steadying the course of trade. Insofar as this view is accepted, it appears at first sight as though the influence of the rate of interest would be weakened. As regards the other category, houses and other dwellings represent the only important type of consumers' capital goods likely to be affected materially by changes in the rate of interest. But the demand for dwellings is clearly dependent also on other factors, notably on the rate at which the number of families is growing in different sections of the community. In view of the trend of our vital statistics it seems probable that we are approaching a phase in which the number of families will cease to grow. It is difficult to suppose that under such conditions the demand for new private dwellings can remain at a very high level, however low the rate of interest may fall. This suggests that one of the major classes of capital expenditure which is susceptible to variations in interest rates may in future represent a much smaller part of our aggregate capital expenditure than it has done in the past. So far as the argument has gone the conclusion would appear to be that the influence of the rate of interest on capital expenditure is limited to certain particular directions, and that its continued efficacy in those directions is threatened by modern tendencies.

The argument, however, is not, as yet, complete. Changes in the rate of interest may affect economic activity through a channel different in kind from any that have hitherto been considered. A fall (or rise) in the rate of interest serves to raise (or lower) the Stock Exchange prices of fixed-interest securities, and has a considerable effect on the prices of most ordinary shares. This may affect the willingness of large sections of the public to purchase goods and services in general. When prices are rising on the Stock Exchange, dealers and speculators make profits, whereas as a body they are apt to make losses when Stock Exchange prices are falling. Many of them expect to make profits over an average of years and regard these profits as a part of their spendable income. When, accordingly, the trend of Stock Exchange prices is upwards, dealers and speculators will feel better able to spend money than when times are bad. Under the heading of speculators in this connection may be included not only professional speculators but a large number of persons who habitually buy and sell shares with a view to capital profits. People who do this are much more numerous nowadays than they used to be, and they probably account for an appreciable fraction of the aggregate purchasing power of the community. Moreover, even people who seldom change their securities are influenced in their state of mind by a rise or fall in their capital value and would be more likely to feel that they can afford a certain piece of expenditure when security prices are rising than when they are falling.

There are grounds for supposing that this particular influence is of considerable and growing importance. It is notorious that a slump or boom on the Stock Exchange quickly affects the demand for certain luxury goods, e.g. the more expensive types of motor-cars. It is fairly well established, again, that the Wall Street crash in 1929 led directly to a substantial curtailment of consumers' purchases. Indeed, this chain of cause and effect supplies one of the most probable explanations of the fact that trade movements are normally more violent in the United States than in Great Britain; for the distinction between income and capital still retains in Great Britain a far greater degree of sanctity than it does in the United States. Thus, in the influence of the rate of interest on security values, and the influence of the level of security values on effective purchasing power, we have a channel of connection which is consistent both with common-sense considerations and the broad facts of recent experience.

A rise in security values, it should be added, may affect businesses as well as private individuals. It will improve the balance-sheet position of a business which holds marketable securities; and it will also make it easier for companies to raise new capital without incurring prior charges. In these ways, businesses might be encouraged to undertake extensions to which a certain risk attached. Conversely, a fall in security values may be an influence making for more cautious business policies.

The minds of many economics students have been feeling their way in recent years towards the tentative conclusions which have been set out above. But it has seemed desirable to some of us at Oxford that a more systematic effort should be made than hitherto to ascertain whether these conclusions, positive and negative alike, are well founded. There has been in existence for some years among the tutors engaged in teaching economics at Oxford a research group which has been investigating the factors affecting the course of economic activity. These investigations cover a considerable range of problems, and the methods include both statistical analysis and interviews and discussions with businessmen. One of the questions examined has been that of the effects of changes in the rate of interest, and a number of leading businessmen, representative of different branches of industry, commerce, and finance, have been closely questioned by us as to the way in which, as they see it, their activities are affected. . . . Broadly, . . . the opinions of the businessmen whom we have examined are in conformity with the argument developed above. The majority deny that their activities have been, or are likely to be, directly affected in any way by changes in interest rates. Of those who take the view that they might sometimes be affected, few suggest that the influence is an important one. This applies, it should be observed, with some qualifications, even to the representatives of the building industry whom we consulted. In at least the majority of cases the negative character of the answers given cannot be attributed to prejudice. It was common to find witnesses who denied that their activities were in any way affected by changes in interest rates, but who, nonetheless, held the view that the rate of interest is an important factor in the economic situation for reasons not easy to ascertain. Still less can the nature of the answers be attributed to misunderstanding or confusion of thought. Our questions were closely pressed and reiterated in different terms, and they covered every possible reaction. Frequently, moreover, in response to our questions, the methods of calculation actually employed in weighing projects of capital expenditure were precisely explained; and these were such as to disregard altogether variations in interest rates.

Our investigations in the Oxford Economists' Research Group have been intensive rather than extensive, and the "sample" of firms consulted is small. Moreover, the sample may be said to be biased in one important respect. The majority of businessmen we have consulted represent prosperous firms in a strong financial position. It may be that changes in interest rates have a greater influence on the actions of businesses which are in financial difficulties. Certainly on general grounds one would expect that such businesses would be more likely to be affected by changes in the ease or stringency of credit conditions, i.e. in the abundance or scarcity of bank money as distinct from the rate charged for it.

It seems fair, however, to claim that our investigations, though not amounting to a conclusive demonstration, confirm with a high degree of probability the negative conclusions which have been tentatively advanced on grounds of common sense, i.e. that the direct influence of variations in the rate of interest on the actions of the majority of businesses of an ordinary industrial or commercial character, either in purchasing materials or in undertaking capital expenditure, is not likely to be very great. Indeed, they go somewhat further than this, and suggest that the influence exerted indirectly through the change in the level of security values and consequently in balance-sheet positions, though of some importance, is not of great importance so far as the actions of businesses are concerned.

Though these conclusions are essentially negative, we think that their publication may contribute, if only by way of clearing the ground, to the constructive development of economic thought. It is of interest, therefore, to consider some of the corollaries which appear reasonable if these conclusions are accepted.

In the first place it would be very rash to infer that the importance of the rate of interest in the working of the economic system has been exaggerated. The economist's presumption that great importance must attach to a factor so fundamental as the rate of interest remains, and should not be lightly dismissed. What emerges is that the role played by the ordinary businessman in the transmission of the effects of interest changes is an essentially passive role. The active agents in the process must be looked for elsewhere; and the directions in which they may be found have already been indicated. Possibly the suggestions conveyed by the general trend of economic analysis in the past have underestimated these other effects of interest changes as much as they have overestimated the direct reactions upon the ordinary businessman.

It was suggested above that the growing vogue of the idea of regulating public works with a view to trade stability might seem calculated to weaken the influence of the rate of interest on the volume of this type of capital expenditure. It may well be, however, that this is a superficial view. One important aspect of all projects of public works expenditure is the budgetary aspect. This is an aspect which is apt to receive only slight attention in economic discussion, largely because of the spread in recent years of the idea that un-balanced budgets may be a useful instrument in recovery from de-pression. But the necessity for governments to balance their budgets over a period of years remains inexorable. Two powerful tendencies are at work today which are likely to make this task increasingly difficult. There is first the unprecedentedly heavy expenditure on arm-aments which is being undertaken in many important countries. Secondly, there is the movement from rapidly growing towards de-clining populations which is in progress throughout the western world, and which is likely in various ways to aggravate budgetary difficulties. In these circumstances it is to be expected that govern-ments in many countries, including particularly Great Britain, will be increasingly preoccupied in future years with the problem of budgetary equilibrium. It follows that the financial aspect of projects of public works is likely to be of crucial importance. Schemes of public works which would entail substantial charges on the national exchequer or on local funds would encounter formidable resistance on financial grounds.

The rate of interest may, therefore, play an extremely important part in determining the volume of public works expenditure which it proves practicable to undertake. There are many types of public works or public utility expenditure which yield an appreciable finan-cial return, which, however, may be insufficient at the prevailing level of interest rates to cover the service of the loan required. If a materially lower level of interest rates could be established, the range of public works which were commercial propositions would be en-larged, and the range which could be undertaken without imposing serious burdens on the budget would also be enlarged. Moreover, a low rate of interest by facilitating a reduction in the annual charge for the national debt contributes directly to balancing the budget, and thus makes it easier to undertake public works schemes which are not fully remunerative but are desirable on general economic grounds. For these reasons it may well prove that a low rate of interest will be of vital importance in the years that lie ahead. It may represent the only means of reconciling the conflict between considerations of economic activity and considerations of financial solvency, neither of which can be disregarded without disaster.

The influence of the rate of interest on the expenditure of private individuals may prove equally great. It has already been suggested that the direct effect of changes in interest rates on the purchase of consumers' capital goods may prove of diminishing importance in future; but that, on the other hand, the indirect effect on general expenditure exerted through Stock Exchange prices may be of increasing importance. If this conclusion is sound, the problem of securing a reasonable stability in Stock Exchange values becomes of central importance in the working of the economic system, and deserves more systematic attention than it has hitherto received.

But there is another aspect of this question which is of great interest to the analytical economist. A generation ago there was much discussion of the question whether a fall in the rate of interest was likely to increase or decrease the volume of saving. The traditional view was that a lower rate of interest would diminish saving, and vice versa. But, discussing the question exclusively in terms of the ability to save and the incentive to save, economists found it increasingly difficult to reconcile this assumption with common sense and general experience, and the discussion ended in a prevailing agreement that the effect of a change in the rate of interest on the volume of saving was about as likely to be in the one direction as the other, and was not likely to be important in either case. The reactions of the rate of interest on security prices have, however, an important bearing on this question. As we have seen, there are substantial grounds for believing that an important section of the public is induced by an upward movement on the Stock Exchange to spend more freely, and consequently, other things being equal, to save less. Indeed, the importance of the rate of interest in the working of the trade cycle may, perhaps, lie as much in its reactions on saving and consumption as in those on investment.

This, however, is a short-period transitional influence, associated with falling rather than with low interest rates. Is it possible that as a long-period proposition also the old-fashioned assumption that a lower rate of interest will check saving and vice versa is more soundly based than economists in the past generation have felt able to assume? This is a question that is likely to prove of great importance to the economic stability of society. For a period which may be fairly prolonged we have before us the prospect of large and increasing armament expenditure. But it seems inevitable that sooner or later we shall be confronted with the necessity of effecting a transition to a new economic equilibrium in which capital expenditure plays a substantially smaller part than it does today. Loan expenditure on rearmament must come to an end eventually. The expenditure of the public on houses cannot be expected to continue at anything like the level of recent years when the number of families has ceased to grow. It is difficult to suppose that expenditure on public works will be undertaken on a scale that will compensate fully for the possible decline in capital expenditure under these two headings. But if the demand for capital goods must be expected to diminish it will be essential, if a prolonged period of economic malaise is to be avoided, to secure a corresponding increase in the demand for ordinary consumers' goods. Indeed, the central economic problem of the next generation may be how this can be effected against the background of difficult budgetary conditions. The problem is formidable in the extreme. The difficulties in the way of an adequate solution are immense. But a solution would become much easier if it could be assumed that the establishment of a materially lower rate of interest would exert an enduring influence on the habits of a large section of the public in regard to expenditure and saving.

ROBERT V. ROSA

Interest Rates and
the Central Bank*

Rosa reaffirms the stabilization power of monetary policy in the new economic environment following World War II. He argues that the downgrading of the role of monetary control that was expressed by many economists in the 1930's and '40's was an exaggerated reaction to the conditions of the depression. In a reevaluation of the subject, he contends that the efficacy of monetary policy probably lies somewhere between the enthusiastic hopes expressed in the pre-1930 period, as exemplified by Keynes, and the belittling of its role

* Reprinted with permission of The Macmillan Co. from *Money, Trade and Economic Growth: in Honor of John Henry Williams* by David McCord Wright and Robert V. Rosa, eds., pp. 270–95. Copyright 1951 by The Macmillan Co.

in the following two decades, as illustrated by the views of Henderson. Rosa suggests that, with the existence of a large public debt, small changes in the interest rate may well be sufficient to exert a powerful influence on the money markets in that they affect the willingness of financial institutions to hold or sell government securities as their prices change. This, in turn, affects their ability to grant loans. The author observes that it is this change in credit availability which can be profoundly influenced by central bank action. If the monetary authorities sell enough securities in the open market to drive interest rates up and the price of bonds down, financial institutions will retain their government bonds rather than accept capital losses. In this way, the quantity of funds available to potential borrowers will be reduced. Rosa has thus shifted the emphasis of monetary policy from the effect of interest rate changes directly on borrowers to its effect on lenders. In this selection, the author supports the widely-held view that monetary policy is likely to be more effective in combating excessive credit expansion and inflation than in offsetting credit contraction and deflation. He also contends that, while fiscal policy has attracted the attention of economists as the more powerful stabilizing tool, monetary policy has the advantage of greater flexibility, in part because the authorities can act without the legislative delay involved with fiscal policy.

Two decades ago it still bordered on heresy to suggest that central bank control over interest rates was useless as a restraint upon cyclical swings in the American economy. Today that heresy has become widely accepted as dogma.[1] But paradoxically the dominant importance acquired by the public debt in World War II has, at once, confirmed the adherents of the new dogma in their views, and raised new prospects for strengthening contra-cyclical credit policy in the United States through variations in interest rates. To those who

[1] For example, see President's Council of Economic Advisers, "Comment Submitted to the Joint Congressional Committee on the Economic Report," *Hearings before the Joint Committee, January 17–20, 1950* (Washington, U. S. Government Printing Office, 1950), especially pp. 63–68. The present writer has commented on the Council's expression of views in a forthcoming review article, "The Revival of Monetary Policy" prepared for publication in the *Review of Economics and Statistics.*

already believed that guided variation in interest rates was largely futile, it was but a final, clinching development that an enlargement of the public debt should seem to narrow the range of permissible rate movement. Yet it may be precisely the conditions that now make it desirable, and possible, to limit rate variation which at the same time offer the central bank an opportunity for effective action.

Presumably, a limitation on the range of interest rate fluctuations is implied by the existence of a large public debt because the rate variations typical in the twenties and earlier would, in the new circumstances, set off a cumulative unloading or acquisition of debt instruments that would have harmful repercussions throughout the economy, and might perhaps (in the event of unloading) impair the Government's credit. It is this fundamental concern, rather than the effect of rate changes on the Treasury's outlays for debt service, that makes a return to widely fluctuating rates unlikely. However, is this not merely to say, when examined in another light, that the securities and credit markets have become much more susceptible than they were years ago to any given change in interest rates? May it not also be significant that the presence of a substantial volume of Government securities in the debt structure, at all maturity periods, gives the central bank a medium through which it can directly influence the prices and yields on securities and credits of all terms? Is it not possible now that relatively small changes in interest rates, initiated or permitted by a central bank capable of reaching any segment of the rate structure, may give general credit policy an influence which it could not exert in the past?

These questions cannot, of course, be answered categorically, but the present paper aims deliberately at exploring the possibilities of an affirmative reply. For this purpose, administrative questions are not relevant; attention centers on the potential applications of central banking policy, not on whether that policy should in practice be administered by the Treasury, the Federal Reserve, or shared between them. It is relevant, but will not be labored here, that the great emphasis of the postwar years upon sustaining high levels of output and employment may itself produce an economic environment with a high susceptibility to inflationary distortions, and their aftermath — an environment in which the marginal influence of changes in credit availability may assume critical importance in finding a balance, from year to year, somewhere between the extremes of rigidity and instability.[2] This paper will limit itself, however, to a re-

[2] Cf. Richard A. Musgrave, "Credit Controls, Interest Rates, and Management of the Public Debt," *Income Employment and Public Policy* (New York, W. W. Norton and Co., 1948), p. 253.

examination of some of the avenues for influencing economic activity through changes in market rates of interest, as these changes may be guided or controlled by the central bank.

At one time it was thought that changes in market rates of interest provided a satisfactory explanation — and central bank control over rates an adequate corrective — for cyclical economic disturbance. But experience proved disappointing. In part, the failings of earlier analysis and policy may be attributed to a misdirection of emphasis. Economists and central banking theorists long believed that the significance of market rates of interest, and of central banking efforts to vary these rates, lay in the effects produced upon *borrowers,* and upon *savers.* Little if any attention was given to *lenders;* their function was considered that of automatic response to central bank action, without any meaningful independent influence on economic behavior. Insofar as writers did attach some importance to changes in the "availability of credit," they failed to see that any general control over changes in credit availability was inseparably linked to changes in interest rates. Consequently, as experience and direct investigation revealed a rather wide range of indifference to rate changes among borrowers, and suggested that saving was closely related to such other factors as changes in income, there was an understandable slackening in the enthusiasm for central bank control over rates as a positive method of moderating cyclical fluctuation.

In part, too, environmental changes can account for the failure of interest rates to arouse the expected response from borrowers and savers during the twenties and thirties. Although both may have been more responsive to interest rate fluctuations in an earlier day, changes were taking place in the debt structure, and in the flow of loanable funds through institutional intermediaries, which increased the independent significance of the lending function in the financing mechanism of the American economy. There was, in effect, a cultural lag between the development of the theory of interest rates and of central banking, on the one hand, and the changing characteristics of the money markets, on the other. Moreover, since the shifts in credit availability which rate changes reflect can be only one of many influences upon the stability of the economy, the significance of changes in lender behavior might well have gone unnoticed by those earlier students who were hoping to find in rate movements and central bank action a complete solution to the problem of cyclical fluctuations.

Now that the leavening phases of exaggerated emphasis, and of reaction and disillusionment, have been passed, it should be useful to attempt a fresh review of the part which interest rate variations effected by the central bank can play in moderating cyclical swings in the American economy, to see where we have come out. This will be attempted here, first, by reviewing a few of the landmarks in the vast literature that has appeared on this question during the first half of the present century; second, by describing the major institutional changes affecting the flow of lendable funds and the money markets in the United States, particularly those occurring since the establishment of the Federal Reserve System in 1914; and third, by discussing the substance of central bank rate action, as applied to short-term rates, long-term rates, and the interrelations between them.

I. THE DEVELOPMENT OF CONCEPTS[3]

From the Wicksell of *Interest and Prices*[4] to the Keynes of the *General Theory*,[5] despite the twists and turns of interest rate and central banking theory at other hands over the intervening years, the main stream of analysis implicitly accepted three underlying propositions. First, a change in rates at the central bank would actually assure a roughly corresponding change at the commercial banks. Second, by focusing attention on "the" interest rate, most writers assumed a synchronous movement throughout the rates on comparable debt instruments of all maturities; that is, a change at the commercial banks was expected to spread throughout the short-term market and on through all other maturities. Third, once rate changes were achieved through central bank action, they would be followed by appropriate action on the part of borrowers (and, most writers would have added, on the part of savers). Only if all three of these presumed relationships were to hold would it be possible to go on further to accomplish precise objectives in terms of the money supply, the price level, and the control of the business cycle.

During the first and second decades of Federal Reserve operations, most American writers supported doctrines similar to those of Wicksell. There was little awareness of the three underlying assumptions implied by such doctrines, nor of possible gaps between concept

---

[3] Dr. Clifton H. Kreps, Jr., of the Research Department of the Federal Reserve Bank of New York, has contributed greatly to this summary of the literature on interest rate and central banking theory.

[4] Knut Wicksell, *Interest and Prices* (London, Macmillan and Co., Ltd., 1936), a delayed translation of *Geldzins und Guterpreise* (Jena, Gustav Fischer, 1898).

[5] J. M. Keynes, *The General Theory of Employment, Interest, and Money* (New York, Harcourt, Brace and Co., 1936).

and reality at any of these three critical stages in the credit process. Such writers as Irving Fisher, having developed the equation of exchange into the quantity theory of money, devoted themselves instead to clarifying the purposes for which the presumably powerful central bank controls should be used. Only the Federal Reserve System itself, facing the concrete problems of implementation, saw the possible gaps and entertained a genuine skepticism over the feasibility of bridging them.

When the reaction against central banking and the significance of interest rates began in the mid-twenties, two writers with broad backgrounds of experience within the System undertook some clarification. Pointing out the exaggerated nature of the claims that had been made for central banking, Burgess in 1927 and Riefler in 1930 showed the limitations existing at each of the three stages which separate central bank action from its end results. A change in discount rate, even when reinforced by the newly discovered use of open market operations, would not automatically induce corresponding rate changes among the commercial banks. Moreover, interest rate changes themselves (once achieved in the market) were regarded as important chiefly "as the outward evidence of changes in underlying credit conditions."[6] Burgess pointed out that ". . . the importance of a change in the discount rate lies principally in its being a public recognition by a group of responsible and well-informed people of a change in the credit situation."[7] Riefler also found that rate changes by the central bank or the commercial banks (appropriately confined to short-term debt by the traditions of the "commercial loan theory") might extend with diminished force, if at all, into the long-term segment of the debt structure.[8]

But the most important controversy appeared at the third stage — the effects of rate changes upon borrowing and saving. Keynes, for

[6] W. R. Burgess, *The Reserve Banks and the Money Market,* first ed. (New York, Harper and Bros., 1927), p. 276. Cf. W. W. Riefler, *Money Rates and Money Markets* (New York, Harper and Bros., 1930), p. xv, ". . . the importance of changes in money rates lies in the underlying readjustments which they connote."

[7] Burgess, *op. cit.,* p. 185. Cf. also the second edition, 1936, p. 221.

[8] Riefler, *op. cit.,* especially pp. 116–123, and p. 218 where he says, "whether the effect of credit policy on money rates . . . could ever seriously affect the level of bond yields . . . raises a question . . . that does not lend itself either to categorical affirmation or denial." The firm position taken by Keynes in *A Treatise on Money,* Vol. II (New York, Harcourt, Brace & Co., 1930), especially pp. 352–362, presents an interesting contrast, since Keynes relies upon Riefler's work for much of his statistical evidence.

example, held in the *Treatise* that only the long-term rate could be effective in bringing saving and investment into equilibrium.[9] And in the *General Theory*, having discovered the tautology which relieved him of concern over a divergence between saving and investment, he still regarded "the" interest rate as the determinant (in conjunction with the marginal efficiency of capital) of private investment.[10] Hawtrey was most prominent among those who placed reliance on the short-term rate, which influenced the working capital investment of traders, and affected saving primarily through the resulting effects of the traders' actions upon the price level.[11] The eventual reaction of many writers to the disputes between "the short-enders and the long-enders" was to disown both. Hicks, for one, had by 1939 come to the position that rate movements within the "ordinary range (say between 2 per cent and 7 per cent per annum) . . ." could have at best only a slight effect upon short-term borrowers; while the longer-term borrowers, who should find their capitalized present values more sharply affected by interest rate changes, would discover that their necessary "risk-allowance will become so large as to wipe out any possible gains."[12]

The Oxford surveys of 1938 and 1940, questioning businessmen concerning the importance of interest rates in their decisions, reinforced Professor Hicks' iconoclasm.[13] But the later of the two questionnaires, better devised and reaching a wider sample of respondents, showed the door opening upon what has become, at least in the United States since World War II, the dominant significance of

[9] Keynes, *Treatise*, II, *op. cit.*, p. 348, and pp. 352–364.

[10] Keynes, *General Theory, op. cit.*, especially chapters 13 through 17.

[11] R. G. Hawtrey, *Currency and Credit* (London, Longmans, Green and Co., 1919), presents in Chapter XIII the earliest form of these views; his subsequent development of them continued through a number of volumes, the latest thorough treatment is in *Capital and Employment* (London, Longmans, Green and Co., 1937).

[12] J. R. Hicks, *Value and Capital* (Oxford, Oxford University Press, 1939), pp. 225–226. Hicks' doubts were anticipated earlier in Williams' review of Keynes' *Treatise*, cf. J. H. Williams, "The Monetary Doctrines of J. M. Keynes," *Quarterly Journal of Economics*, XLV, No. 4, August 1931, especially pp. 575–584.

[13] H. D. Henderson, "The Significance of the Rate of Interest," *Oxford Economic Papers*, October 1938, I, pp. 1–13; J. E. Meade and P. W. S. Andrews, "Summary of Replies to Questions on Effects of Interest Rates," same volume, pp. 14–31. And R. S. Sayers, "Business Men and the Terms of Borrowing," *Oxford Economic Papers*, March 1940, III, pp. 23–31; P. W. S. Andrews, "A Further Inquiry into the Effects of Rates of Interest," same volume, pp. 32–73.

interest rates and of central bank controls. Roughly a quarter of the replies indicated that the *availability* of bank credit, or of funds obtained through the securities markets, affected businessmen's decisions to make (or the *timing* of their decisions to make) expenditures upon new plant, or upon repairs and maintenance, or upon inventories.[14] It follows, although the Oxford writers did not draw this conclusion from their own data, that if changes in various market rates of interest exert an important influence upon the extent to which *lenders* make funds available, those rates will have some appreciable influence upon economic activity.

Although Burgess and Riefler both saw that rates and credit availability were reflections of each other, rather than separate compartments of the financial mechanism, it was not until 1941 that the full relevance of this fact to monetary policy began to emerge in published discussion, notably in Professor Williams' address at the annual meetings of the American Economic Association.[15] From that point on, largely through an oral medium, without benefit of a published written record, Williams has taken the leadership in focusing attention on the lenders, and on the significance of interest rates as a symptom of the factors causing a tightening or loosening in the new credit made available by lenders.[16] In essence, it is not necessarily interest rates as a cost to the borrower, nor as an inducement to the saver, but rather interest rates as a reflection of underlying changes in credit availability, that have an important (though certainly not always a decisive) impact upon the generation of business cycles. The changed character of the debt and the changes in the flow of loanable funds — which have raised this aspect of interest rates to new prominence and have created a high degree of market sensitivity to influences reflected in relatively slight movements of rates — are described in the following section.

[14] Andrews, "A Further Inquiry . . . ," *op. cit.*, pp. 35–37, cf. also Sayers, *op. cit.*, pp. 23 and 28.

[15] J. H. Williams, "The Implications of Fiscal Policy for Monetary Policy and the Banking System," *Proceedings of the American Economic Association*, Part 2, XXXII, No. 1, March 1942, reprinted in *Postwar Monetary Plans and Other Essays*, 3rd ed. (New York, A. A. Knopf, 1947), especially pp. 98–103.

[16] One of the few published expressions of this same point of view appears in F. A. Lutz, "The Interest Rate and Investment in a Dynamic Economy," *American Economic Review*, December 1945, XXXV, No. 5, especially pp. 828–830. Professor Paul McCracken, formerly Director of Research, Federal Reserve Bank of Minneapolis, developed similar views in his paper, "The Present Status of Monetary and Fiscal Policy," *The Journal of Finance*, March 1950, V, No. 1, pp. 24–39.

II. CHANGING CHARACTERISTICS OF THE CREDIT SYSTEM

The fundamental structural changes affecting the significance of central bank control over interest rates have themselves, in turn, resulted from many causes. For present purposes those causes are not relevant. What matters is that the size and composition of the net debt of the economy, the institutional channels through which resources pass into the holdings of that debt, and the organization of the markets in which debt instruments are bought and sold, have all changed considerably since the Federal Reserve System began operations in 1914. It is important to identify the major developments, and to interpret their consequences for effective central bank action.

A. *The Major Developments* [17]

(1) *The "supply" of debt instruments.* In 1914, it was roughly correct to say that all of the ultimate net debt of the economy embodied some degree of credit risk.[18] The general public could choose between holding cash and holding risk assets; and the commercial banks in turn held risk assets, in large measure, as the collateral supporting the bank deposits which represented most of the cash. The calculus of the choice between cash (or idle reserves) and risk assets involved not only liquidity preference (with its complex of determining motives), but also an allowance for credit risk. Yet it was the "pure" rates with which the prevailing theory, and the prescriptions for central bank action, were concerned. Not until a form of debt instrument free of credit risk should become a dominant part of the total debt, extending through a representative selection of all maturities, would it be possible to distinguish sharply the effects of time and liquidity preference (net of the credit risk factors) for a given money supply at a given point in time. Moreover, only then would it be possible for market forces to reveal unambiguously (through comparison with the schedule of rates free of credit risk) the magnitude of risk differentials among various types of debt, and perhaps to point up the significance of efforts to influence the risk premium itself.

---

[17] The data used in this section on changes in the composition of total debt and in the distribution of debt holdings are derived from an unpublished study of the American debt structure from 1914 to 1948 which A. J. R. Smith of Harvard University is bringing to completion as this is written.

[18] Only 1.5 per cent of total net debt was in U. S. Government securities, and most of these securities were lodged in the reserves held by national banks against their note issues.

By the end of World War II, such an environment had been created as a result of the enormous growth of the public debt. Total net debt in the United States, both public and private, was roughly 65 billion dollars in 1914. It had doubled by 1919; tripled by 1929; emerged about the same as a decade earlier by 1939; and was more than six times the 1914 figure by 1948. Meanwhile the proportion of Federal Government securities in the total had grown from 1.5 per cent in 1914 to 50.4 per cent in 1948. Short-term debt, which the traditions of the commercial loan theory made the special province of commercial banks, had shrunk from 40.9 per cent of total net debt in 1914 to 30.0 per cent in 1948; and the proportion of Government securities in the total of short-term debt had risen from a negligible figure to nearly one third.[19] Among the short-term debt instruments used actively for bank reserve adjustments in the New York money market, Government securities had risen from a volume of virtually no significance in 1914 to about one sixth of the total in 1924, and to more than nine tenths of the total in 1948.

(2) *The "demand" for debt instruments.* By 1948, the choice confronting any lender was no longer between cash and the short- or long-term debt instruments of private borrowers, but among cash, Government securities of all practicable maturities, and the debt of private individuals or corporations. And certain institutional changes, marked by the channeling of loanable resources into highly specialized investment concerns, had made lenders acutely sensitive to slight changes in the yield differentials among alternatives, both short and long. A steadily growing popular insistence on "security" — the avoidance of loss, at the expense of accepting lesser yields — had favored the growth of conservative intermediary institutions, operating on relatively narrow margins, and alert to small changes among the yields on debt instruments that would have been considered trivial a few decades earlier. While statistical pitfalls in double-counting challenge any effort to describe accurately the growing "institutionalization of savings" in the United States, there is a basis for very rough generalization. It appears that in 1914 more than one half of the ultimate net debt was held directly by the corporations or individuals providing the resources. By 1948, barely one quarter of the ultimate debt was held directly, the remainder was held through financial intermediaries.

---

[19] For technical reasons, Smith has defined short-term debt as that with original maturity under one year. The well-known defects of such a definition for current money market analysis do not apply, however, in the study of long-run trends.

(3) *Organization and mechanics of the money market*.[20] The changing composition of the debt and the shifting distribution of debt holding were accompanied by a third set of changes of major significance. The organized markets through which issuers or sellers and purchasers or holders of debt were brought together also adapted themselves to the altered character of the supply and demand for debt instruments. During the twenties and thirties, trading in Government securities became increasingly specialized in an over-the-counter market among dealers, and transactions through the stock exchange dwindled to insignificance. By the middle thirties the principal dealers themselves had become part of an informal market organization in which the Federal Reserve Bank of New York, as agent for the Federal Open Market Committee, exerted an increasingly influential role. And as the market demand became more and more sensitive to slight changes in rates, both as among various types of Government securities and between Governments and the debt instruments (including loans) of the private sector, the mechanics of market quotation also reflected the change.

For example, throughout the twenties (and until they disappeared temporarily from use in 1934) certificates, the Government's one-year debt instrument, were traded in terms of price per 100 dollars of par value, just as bonds are traded today. The unit of price change was in thirty-seconds, that is, roughly equivalent to 3 cents per 100 dollars of par value. And the spreads between bid and offer quotations, representing the cost of turnaround sale and repurchase, were rarely less than $\frac{2}{32}$ (or 6 cents per 100 dollars), often rising to $1\frac{0}{32}$ (about 30 cents per 100 dollars). Month-to-month variations in effective yield were frequently $\frac{1}{2}$ of 1 per cent even during relatively tranquil periods, becoming much greater in the event of disturbance. Having been reintroduced as a market instrument in 1942, certificates are no longer quoted on a price basis but in fine graduations of yield. Use is now made of "basis points" of $\frac{1}{100}$ each (corresponding to one cent per 100 dollars). Price spreads, instead of ranging from 6 cents to 30 cents, are usually about 2 cents on the longer certificates; in actual trading, markets are often narrowed to one.[21] The month-to-month yield variation in placid periods is now

[20] Arthur Willis, Special Assistant in the Securities Department, Federal Reserve Bank of New York, contributed greatly to the preparation of this section and of section III B below.

[21] Of course, the spread and the customary quotation changes continue to increase with wider market swings (and greater uncertainty), but the range of variation has shrunk to an order of magnitude fundamentally different from that of the period 1917–32, when certificates were first in use on a substantial scale.

customarily in the neighborhood of $\frac{1}{16}$ of 1 per cent, or even less, instead of $\frac{1}{2}$, with other fluctuations correspondingly narrowed.

Changes of comparable significance have occurred in the bond market over this same period, and have been reflected as well in the market which grew up for Treasury bills (i..e., three-month instruments) after they were first introduced in the United States at the end of 1929. As a corollary of these changing characteristics in the market pricing of Governments, underwriters' bidding and the sale of new issues of corporate and municipal bonds or debentures during recent years have also developed a sensitivity to very small changes. Successful bidding has, since the end of the war, often depended on differences in the third decimal place of an intended yield.[22] It is such changes in customary market practices which indicate, more convincingly than abstract analysis, that the increasing relative importance of Government securities, and the growing concentration of investible funds in the hands of yield-conscious institutions, have made the money markets highly susceptible to slight changes in interest rates.

B. *The Consequences for Central Bank Action*

The paradoxical result of the major developments just described has been to create an environment in which the three unstated premises of Wicksellian theory became, with important modifications, finally fulfilled. These premises, as noted above, fitted the three stages between action by the central bank and eventual reaction by the economy: (1) the direct effect of central bank action upon commercial banks and their loan rates; (2) the fluidity between short-term banking rates and long-term rates; and (3) the influence of the tightening or loosening of credit, as reflected in market rate changes, upon significant economic decisions — to borrow for capital expenditure, to save, or to lend. These developments also raise new questions concerning possible limitations on the effectiveness of central bank action, and alter materially the use which can be made of changes in reserve requirements to affect the availability of bank credit.

(1) *The direct impact of central bank action.* While the central bank has used, and continues to use, the discount rate as a direct influence upon the cost of credit at commercial banks, and as a sym-

[22] One bidding early in 1950 for some short-term bonds went to the fourth decimal place. A bid at net interest cost to the borrower of 1.7181 was successful over a bid of 1.7184. *The New York Times,* March 22, 1950, p. 39. And there have been several similar cases.

bol to the economy of a general change in the economic weather and of central bank policy, the new environment now provides the central bank with direct access to the going rate structure as well. It is no longer sufficient to consider the effects of the discount rate upon commercial bank borrowing from the central bank, the effects of that borrowing upon bank rates and the money supply, and the effects of those in turn upon the entire level and structure of interest rates.[23] For open market operations in Government securities bring the central bank into contact not only with the volume of available bank reserves, but also with the portfolios of all classes of lenders. Open market purchases may not only increase the primary reserves of the commercial banking system, but also the loanable funds of private investors who have sold Governments; and as a counterpart of such a change in the volume of funds potentially available for new commitments, some or all interest rates may decline. Conversely, System sales, or merely an unwillingness to purchase, may drive down the prices of Government securities as potential lenders attempt to acquire fresh funds by unloading Governments, and the associated rise in rates will signify a growing tightness in credit availability.

(2) *Interrelations between short-term and long-term rates.* Because of the relatively high proportion of Government debt to total debt, at all relevant maturities, the behavior of prices for Government securities will directly influence the actual availability of credit for alternative uses (at each maturity) and virtually determine the approximate level of "basic" yields, as well as the direction of change in yields. And the prices of all Governments can be reached (or allowed to move without offsetting interference) through the System's open market operations. Effective central bank action is no longer limited to the roundabout results achieved through influencing the indebtedness of commercial banks (or the reverse — the volume of their excess reserves). Moreover, there is no longer any impediment to a substantial flow of resources back and forth between the short-term and long-term markets. Such switches, compounded of judgments concerning both the economic situation and the market intentions of the System authorities, have not only become a commonplace,

---

[23] Moreover, the influences resulting from changes in the discount rate itself can no longer be limited to this causal sequence. Discount rate changes serve, in effect, to signal a change in the boundaries upon fluctuations in short-term open market rates, and in the prices of Federal Funds, thereby giving particular emphasis when necessary to developments associated with open market operations.

they have actually degenerated into a disruptive "playing the pattern of rates" on several occasions during and following World War II.

Moreover, the commercial banks themselves are no longer confined to short-term obligations; more than one half the earning assets of the member banks in 1948 carried maturities beyond one year, while the estimated proportion in 1914 was one sixth. Not only longer-term Government securities, but also term loans and amortized mortgages, accounted for this shift in the direct impact of the banks upon the longer-term market.

Clearly, through the medium of Government securities and the lengthened term distribution of "bankable" private debt, a real fluidity is imparted to movements between the short-term and long-term markets. And while it may generally be expected that longer-term yields will not shift as swiftly as the shorter-terms in response to the changes in credit availability associated with day-to-day variations in the economic outlook, the long-term market will definitely be influenced by any sustained ease or tightening in the short-term market. The first two of Wicksell's implicit premises have, therefore, been reasonably well satisfied.

(3) *Rate changes and the decisions to borrow, to save, or to lend.* There is little doubt that Wicksell, his contemporaries, and his followers, exaggerated the direct significance of market rates of interest as cost elements affecting decisions to borrow for investment; the niceties of logical refinement, in isolating any one variable for marginal analysis, frequently result in an excess of zeal for the influence of the variable studied. Nonetheless, Wicksell had more on his side than recent critics have allowed. Interest rates do have some importance as a cost factor, particularly with respect to the timing of decisions concerning changes in inventory or plant where the ratio of stocks to sales, or of equipment to sales, is relatively high.

So far as saving is concerned, it may well be income and a host of other factors that dominate the decisions of individuals, rather than changes in the inducement offered by interest rates. But a phenomenon little noticed by the Wicksellians has come to overshadow personal savings in importance in the United States. Business savings, gross or net, have generally exceeded personal savings in recent years. And the critical decision as to whether or not to pay out dividends, or retain profits for internal use, may be materially affected by changes in interest rates. In general, rising rates encourage a greater financing of internal expansion through retained earnings; that is, rising rates tend to increase savings.

But it is the lender, neglected by the monetary theorists, who does most to put new substance in the older doctrine. As Part III will indicate in further detail, rate changes brought about by the open market operations of the central bank influence the disposition or the ability of lenders to make funds available to borrowers, either for the continuation of outstanding indebtedness or for incurring new debt to finance expansion.

(4) *Limitations upon central bank action.* In addition to the obvious fact that interest rates and credit availability alone cannot determine the level of economic activity, and can at best exert but one set of pressures among many, there are two major limitations upon the use which can be made of central bank control over rates. First, the Treasury has an inevitable bias toward low, and relatively constant, interest rates on the Government debt; it faces both the budgetary necessity of holding down the aggregate burden of debt service, and the managerial responsibility for continually refinancing annual maturities that now constitute about ⅕ of the outstanding public debt. Second, although business decisions to retain earnings may to some extent be indirectly influenced by changes in interest rates (as already noted), the secular growth in internal financing (particularly among manufacturing corporations) tends to insulate many businesses from the direct effects of changes in credit availability.

Neither need be a debilitating limitation, however. So far as the Treasury is concerned, it can give up the comforts of low and constant yields in periods when these are attainable only by releases of Federal Reserve credit that would result in inflationary expansion and a sustained depreciation in the purchasing power of the dollar. Moreover, with the money markets sensitive to small changes in interest rates, it is not likely that the Treasury would ever have to face wide swings in its issuing rates. Whatever swings occur may, furthermore, offset each other over time. A rise in rates associated with tighter credit will presumably be followed by rate reductions in periods of ease, so that although the Treasury's interest charge on current refinancing may vary from year to year, the long-time average of the debt burden need not necessarily be altered materially under a flexible program of central banking control over credit and rates.

While some segments of the economy may be more nearly independent of outside financing than was true in the earlier years of this century, the influence of changes in credit availability for the economy as a whole remains significant. There probably is, as suggested earlier, some marginal interrelationship between the current behavior of the money markets and business decisions to retain profits; in general, rising rates (or a heightened state of uncertainty) should stimulate the retention of earnings. Even if there were no such relationship, the implied market judgment of the business outlook, associated with changes in interest rates and credit availability, will itself (along with other factors) exert some influence upon business decisions to expand capacity or output, or to postpone such action. Further, there still remain large sectors of the economy which depend heavily upon the credit available from lenders. Much of the construction industry, and a high proportion of railroad and public utility investment, for example, require substantial outside financing;[24] the same is true for most wholesalers and retailers.

(5) *Interest rates and changes in reserve requirements.* There is another implication for credit control in the widespread holding of the public debt — an implication which has not yet been fully appreciated. That is, changes in reserve requirements have now become a poor substitute for open market operations in exerting a contra-cyclical influence upon the availability of bank credit. For when all banks hold large portfolios of Government securities, which they regard as the closest substitute for excess reserves, a change in requirements may have no more than a moderate psychological effect upon the bank credit extended to private borrowers. Instead, a higher requirement, for example, may lead mainly to a shift of Governments from the banks into the Federal Reserve, *unless* interest rates on the Governments are allowed to rise as the Federal Reserve "backs away" from the securities being offered to it. Because of the large volume of Government securities now wedged between bank reserve balances and their private credits, open market operations, rather than the blunt impact of changes in reserve requirements, provide the most flexible and effective method for bringing about changes in the availability of credit in the highly sensitive money markets that have evolved over recent years.

Thus, it is a mistake to suppose that changes in the reserve requirements applicable to member banks can, in the new environment created by a large public debt, effectively accomplish a material change in the availability of short-term (or of long-term) bank credit

[24] Cf. A. G. Hart, *Money, Debt and Economic Activity.* (New York, Prentice Hall, Inc., 1948), p. 181, where he says that the direct influence of interest rates as costs is significant in these industries, and adds that "these lines almost always account for well over one-half of investment."

without affecting interest rates.[25] If reserve requirements are raised while at the same time the central bank is attempting to hold the interest rates on Government securities constant, there will be an ample flow of new central bank credit to absorb all of the Governments which the banks wish to unload; there must be, to prevent a price decline. In that event, there will simply be a reduction in the volume of bank-held Government securities (corresponding closely to the amount of the added reserve requirements) and a parallel rise in central bank purchases, without any necessarily significant effect upon the extension of private credit. Tightening can only be achieved through an increase in reserve requirements if that action is carried out as a form of open market operations, with the Federal Reserve, in effect, forcing the banks to meet the requirements either by selling their Government securities to nonbank investors, or by curtailing their private credits. To do that, the Federal Reserve must be able to lower the prices at which it purchases Government securities. The desired degree of tightness can no doubt be obtained with a relatively small price (rate) change — so small, perhaps, as superficially to appear trivial. But the potency of such a change comes from the impact of "uncertainty" upon markets dominated by sensitive investors; and there can be no uncertainty if the central bank is committed in advance to pegged support of Government securities at the prices and rates attached to those securities when they were issued in the past.

Nor can the inevitable link between changes in credit availability and changes in interest rates be broken by a compromise approach — compelling member banks to hold interest-earning Government securities instead of additional reserve balances, in the event of a rise (for example) in reserve requirements. For so long as banks hold a substantial volume of Government securities outside the security-reserve, marginal changes in the credit available at the banks will depend on possible shifts between their "free" Government securities and other debt instruments. Only if rates are permitted to rise, can credit extension based on the funds obtained through sale of the "free" Government securities be restrained. The effective restraint would still be that imposed by the rate changes (and by expectations of rate changes). To attempt to avoid the fundamental interrelationship between rates on Government securities and the general availability of bank credit by freezing *all* bank holdings of

[25] Contrast the view expressed in President's Council of Economic Advisers, *op. cit.*, p. 68.

Governments into such reserves would be impractical and grossly inequitable. The proportions of Government securities held by the various individual banks differ widely, ranging roughly from 20 per cent to 80 per cent of total deposits. Even if such a freeze were feasible, fresh credit could still be provided by all lenders other than member banks so long as the Federal Reserve were purchasing freely the Government securities offered for sale by other lenders. And each sale of Governments to the central bank by nonbank lenders would, in turn, increase the reserves of the banking system — permitting multiple bank credit expansion upon these reserves unless the central bank could reabsorb them through open market sales (an unlikely expedient if short- and long-term security prices were being supported).

It appears impossible, therefore, to use reserve requirements (whether applied to reserve balances or to a security-reserve) as an effective direct control over credit availability, *unless* interest rates can move to express the intended tightening (or loosening) of credit. Any effective control must always come back to interest rates. No mechanical contrivance, aimed at immobilizing a part of commercial bank portfolios, can effect a short-cut around the variable interest rates which accompany changes in credit availability. The place for changes in reserve requirements, under postwar conditions, would seem to be largely that of effecting long-run structural adjustments in the ultimate reserves of the banking system, not in independently attempting the contra-cyclical regulation of credit availability, a function better served by open market operations (with changes in the discount rate giving emphasis to particular market developments).

III. THE SCOPE OF CENTRAL BANK ACTION

The views expressed in this paper represent a reaction against a reaction; they do not by any means, however, imply a return to the original conception of central bank rate policy as the touchstone of economic stability. Through its effects upon lenders, and in lesser measure through its effects upon borrowing and upon saving, the central bank action that is possible through interest rate flexibility can, however, exert some moderating restraint upon cyclical swings in the economy. The possibilities for purposeful action may conveniently be considered under three headings: short-term rates, long-term rates, and the relationship between short- and long-term rates.

A. *Short-term Rates*

Because short-term securities and loans usually comprise the greatest proportion of resources "on the move," central bank action will generally be concentrated on short-term rates. For the same reason, changes in the behavior and expectations of lenders will most frequently be reflected in the short-term sector. Short-term rates will, therefore, customarily be the first to register a change in the underlying credit situation — whether that change has originated with the Federal Reserve or with the private sector, or both. Fluctuations in the short-term rates on Government securities are consequently important not only for their effect in increasing or decreasing the attractiveness of alternative short-term loans or investments, but also as a signal of possible further changes throughout longer-term segments of the rate structure. A decline, however slight, if sustained for any appreciable length of time will create uncertainty over the possibility that credit may be turning generally easier, and that other rates may also fall. A rise may set off an opposite chain of expectations. And oftentimes the mere indication of a change in the direction of rate movements may be enough to transform many of the dominant institutions from willing to reluctant lenders, or the reverse. Or, given a gradual development of small rate changes, in an upward direction for example, one more slight twist of the screw may be sufficient to deter a lender's commitment of funds, turning him toward the relative security of a short-term Government issue until the growing uncertainty shall have cleared away.

The pattern of lender reactions need not necessarily be the same for a change of the same direction, or the same magnitude, at two different points in time. The one assured fact is that lenders will always be sensitive to slight changes, careful to balance the possible capital loss (or gain) resulting from a rise (or reduction) in rates against the possibilities of a greater (or lower) yield. But because lenders cannot always be expected to take the same steps following a given rate change, the System's open market account cannot be operated according to a formula. Operations must instead be based on continuous close study of the money markets. Achievement of a desired degree of ease or of restraint will depend heavily on the ability of the central bank officials to "play by ear." And the supreme advantage of open market operations for this purpose is that they can proceed in small steps,[26] where appropriate; they need not be accom-

---

[26] There are a number of technical devices which may strengthen the effect of a simple change in rates. For example, a mere widening of the spread between

panied by formal announcements of intentions, with the rigidity and the possible exaggerated emphasis inherent in such announcements; and they can be readily reversed if the desired response is attained more quickly than expected, or in the event of a subsequent change in the underlying market situation. When emphasis upon a particular rate change is required, both for its direct market impact and its psychological repercussions, the Reserve Banks can compliment the effect of their open market operations upon short-term rates by changing their discount rates.

The effects of these short-rate changes are threefold. First, they enable the central bank to absorb or to release reserve funds on its own initiative, thereby altering the general supply of funds available for credit expansion. Second, they cause a change in the willingness of lenders to make funds available for short-term private credits — not, for example, because a rise of ⅛ of 1 per cent in the bill rate will shut off all other loans being made at 2, or 3, or 4 per cent, but because the uncertainty over further rises will cause hesitation, an unwillingness to go all the way in a new commitment if rates may be generally higher a few weeks later on, a shortening in commitment terms, and a general desire "to wait and see." Third, short-rate changes immediately affect expectations concerning the long-term market, and carry over directly into that market if they are sustained, thereby exerting an important effect upon the timing of lenders' long-term commitments (and of lenders' decisions to switch between long-term Governments and private issues).

B. Long-term Rates

In addition to influencing the movement of long-term rates, and expectations concerning the future behavior of long rates, through changes in the short-term sector, the central bank may also exert its influence directly upon the prices of long-term securities. Prices were, of course, effectively pegged by the support program initiated during the last war. The measures since taken to unloosen these rigid pegs have themselves resulted, in effect, in central bank guidance of the rate levels. Moreover, it seems inevitable that rate changes in the long-term sector, just as in the short, must henceforth be a reflection of central bank policy, regardless of the actual factors setting off such

the System's buying and selling rates on bills may discourage sales to the System Account from lenders' portfolios. But such devices, while essentially corroborating the thesis of this paper, involve details of market mechanics that are outside the scope of this discussion.

change, and regardless of any desire there might be to avoid placing such rate responsibility in the central bank.

The choice is not between central bank control and reliance upon "free market prices," but among alternative uses of the inherent power imposed upon the central bank by the existence of the large public debt. That power will be exercised, whether consciously or unconsciously; and whether by the Treasury or the Federal Reserve. The need is for purposeful direction, based upon an understanding of the influences which changes in long-term rates may bring about.

Already the postwar experience suggests that yield changes of scarcely ⅛ of 1 per cent for the longest-term bonds have considerable market effects.[27] A rise in long-term rates, initiated to reinforce a tightened credit policy, tends to exert a restraining influence upon the lending policies of banks and other lenders, particularly with respect to term loans, thereby slowing up the business expansion dependent upon longer-term financing. The market pricing of new security issues is also immediately affected, and new issues may for a time be held back, leading in some cases to indefinite postponement. As dealers encounter difficulty in retailing issues already "on the shelves," their receptiveness to new issues is notably chilled. At the very least, a greater "spacing-out" of new issues results, in comparison to the flow that would otherwise have occurred. An even sharper effect is exerted upon lenders' attitudes toward mortgages. With most mortgages now carrying conventional interest rates, kept in place by the influence of various guarantee arrangements, any appreciable evidence of an upward trend in long-term rates is associated with an immediate tightening in the availability of mortgage credit. Moreover, any resulting rise in effective mortgage rates (outside the relatively rigid guarantee programs) will raise the total costs of new building to the borrower considerably, since the financing cost is normally a high proportion of the total. Potential borrowers and builders may, therefore, also be discouraged by the rise in (unguaranteed) mortgage rates which usually follows an increase in yields on Government securities, as well as by the reduced availability of mortgage funds.

Conversely, a lowering of yields on long-term Government securities has appreciably stimulative effects. Banks are encouraged to take some of the resulting capital gains on their long-term Govern-

[27] For a review of the actual experience in a limited use of the new central bank influence since World War II, see Mr. Sproul's article, *Changing Concepts of Central Banking*, in this volume.

ment bonds, placing the proceeds in credits to private borrowers. The impetus to the desired bank action may be somewhat weaker in the case of rate reductions than of rate increases, particularly after very low rates have been in effect over a long period. But the initial effect at the time of the rate reduction (provided the economy is not in a state of panic, or utter collapse) can be important. A yield reduction will also usually lead to aggressive purchases of non-Government securities by most lenders, clearing the dealers' shelves of old issues that may have been hard to sell previously, and opening the way for ready financing of newly arising (or previously postponed) issues, as the carrying capacity of dealers is increased by their unloading of old inventories. A comparable stimulus will be given to mortgage financing.

The market conditions governing such changes in yields, so long as the direction and extent of further change is uncertain, will alternately discourage or encourage potential borrowers, who depend upon receptive and favorable markets for obtaining the outside debt financing which their new undertakings require.[28]

The calculus confronting conservative lenders, alert to fractional differences in their portfolio earnings and portfolio values, can be readily illustrated by a few simple computations in investment mathematics. Suppose, for example, that a term structure of rates on Government securities roughly comparable to the 1948 yield curve had been prevailing for some period of time. That is, yields would have been running from 1¼ per cent on Government bonds within one year of call date to 2½ per cent on similar issues extending 20 years to call. A uniform rise of ⅛ of 1 per cent in the market yields throughout this curve would present lenders with the following typical calculations. A newly issued 20-year Government bond, bearing a coupon rate of 2½ per cent, would drop 1¹⁵⁄₁₆ per cent below par; the capital loss on sale would be about $19.40 per $1,000. A similar bond with the same coupon, purchased on the old yield curve when it had 15 years to run, would fall about $15.60 per $1,000 (par

[28] A brief market note in *The New York Times* for January 28, 1950, p. 20, clearly illustrates the possibilities of this modest type of influence: "Market uncertainties have held hazards for the flotation of new issues of both bonds and stocks this week and sentiment in Wall Street is on the cautious side for the period immediately ahead. The continued drift in the prices of Government securities, with several of the shorter-term obligations hovering around 'par' has taken from the bond market much of the buoyant character of a couple of weeks ago. Two substantial issues of securities had to be repriced by underwriting syndicates this week to get by the 'no sale' block."

value). The same type of bond, purchased at the previous rates with 10 years to run, would fall $12.50 per $1,000 (par value). These capital losses would be roughly doubled if the yield curve rose by ¼ of 1 per cent instead of by ⅛, and would be nearly four times as great with an upward shift in the yield curve of ½ of 1 per cent. The capital losses on the 20-year bond, for example, would be approximately 4 and 8 per cent, respectively, of the principal amount.

To shift from such bonds into a higher yield (and presumably relatively safe) short-term private loan would require a rate differential sufficiently large to absorb this capital loss, with something left over to make the shift attractive. Or to shift into an alternative long-term private investment would require a yield sufficiently high, after allowance for a necessary risk differential, to cover the writing off of the capital loss on the lender's sale of his Government bond, and to produce a gain in average net income over time.[29]

Of course, the converse also follows: a stimulus to sales, and to the transfer of resources into other alternatives, would be provided by reductions in the yields on Government bonds. For simplicity, it may be sufficient to consider the capital gain on a 20-year (2½ per cent) Government bond, following yield reductions from the original yield curve described above. A yield decline of ⅛ of 1 per cent would provide a capital gain of nearly 2 per cent; a decline of ¼, a gain of 4 per cent in sale price; and a decline of ½, a gain of about 8½ per cent in price over the principal amount of the original purchase. Lenders may, of course, when confronted by such prospects, merely sell long Governments to obtain the capital gain and go back into short Governments to await better yields in the long-term sector, with no apparent increase in the credit currently available to the private economy. This is one form of the possible abuses of "rate playing"; but undesirable rate playing can be checked (if it should occur in more than a few isolated instances) by encouraging wider fluctuations in short rates, thereby injecting greater uncertainty into the short end of the yield curve. Moreover, this is not a usual phenomenon. The actual result, if declining rates are at all likely to continue,

---

[29] There is also a widespread phobia concerning capital losses on security sales that is of some significance currently, although it may eventually disappear. In numerous instances, even among large lending institutions, a mathematical demonstration of the long-run gain from such switches is rejected because the impact of the capital loss on current income is considered too great. Thus a slight rise in yields on Governments may "freeze in" many current holders who would readily have shifted from Governments into new loans or investments had the yield on Governments been pegged.

will no doubt be that many lenders tempted to unload their long Governments will switch into another block of long-term debt instruments — real estate mortgages, utility bonds, term loans (and direct placements) or the bonds of manufacturing and trade corporations. Moreover, a freshening of demand for these issues creates a favorable climate for the offering of more, and even borrowers who may consider interest rates of no significance to their own decisions will be activated by the evidence of an increased availability of long-term funds.

No doubt the restraint or the stimulus provided to credit expansion through changes in long-term rates will never turn the course of economic activity alone. But rate changes can certainly exert some influence upon the flow of funds and the timing of new undertakings. If not consciously controlled, or worse still, if irrevocably "pegged," the long-term market will inevitably add cumulative force to any major cyclical swings of the economy. Properly guided — not with central bank pinpointing of rates, but with central bank action at critical junctures to bring about changes in the direction and pace of rate movements — the long-term market can, by spacing the flow of funds into longer-term investment opportunities, make a positive contribution toward lessening the amplitude of booms and depressions.

C. *The Relation between Short- and Long-term Rates*

Most of the interrelations between short- and long-term rates that would affect the decisions of lenders have necessarily been described in the preceding sections; neither end of the rate structure can be discussed as a closed compartment. There is, however, another important aspect of the interrelationship which remains to be clarified. Emphasis has been placed throughout this analysis upon the great significance of small changes — the creation of some uncertainty, a simple reversal in direction of change, or a small change in magnitude — as influences upon lender behavior. The implications of such an analysis for changes in long-term rates may be intuitively convincing, for their effects upon capital values are demonstrable and impressive; and the great pressure of demand from the dominant lenders (many of whom must satisfy an actuarial type of income requirement) will create a keen sensitivity to slight variations in yield. But granting that only moderate changes in long rates are, in present circumstances, likely to be permitted, and that within this range an effective influence can be exerted upon lenders through small rate changes, does this not also imply a low ceiling on possible fluctuations of short-term rates? And if so, will not the principal lenders soon come to realize that the range of movement for short-term rates is very narrow indeed, and that the significance of any uncertainty arising from changes within this slender band is relatively trivial?

Such skepticism is prompted, of course, by the characteristic yield curve to which lenders became accustomed over the decade of the forties, when the gently upward sloping schedule that was frozen in by central bank action at the beginning of the war eventually acquired in some circles the status of "natural" permanence. But there is no necessity for mtaintaining the differentials of the recent past. The differentials suitable for bringing about a change in the market will depend upon the underlying supply and demand for funds, and upon the intensity and speed of the central bank's action to tighten or loosen credit. There is no inherent structural reason why short-term rates should not reach or exceed the long-terms in periods that require a vigorous tight money policy; the short-term nature of such a rise would deter any wholesale unloading of longs by investors who would like to "cash in" on a brief period of high short rates. Moreover, changes in the spread between the shortest and longest rates can, in appropriate circumstances, be as much a part of the central bank's rate policy as the individual changes of such rates themselves. And in general, of course, so long as short rates remain below the long, the narrower the spread between them the less will be the inducement for lenders to commit funds for a long period.

Furthermore, the shape of the yield curve extending from the shortest to the longest yields may be expected to vary with the effects of tighter or easier credit conditions. One of the first effects of a vigorous tight money program might, for example, be a flattening of the yield curve. That would, if brought about rapidly, make intermediate bonds somewhat more attractive than longer issues to investors disposing of newly arising funds, thereby rendering credit unavailable to some potential long-term borrowers. It would at the same time tend to "block in" existing holders of the intermediate Governments by eliminating the large appreciation in capital value which such bonds would otherwise acquire through the passage of time under the typical sloping yield curve.

So far as the effectiveness of central bank action upon short-term rates is concerned, the relative constancy of the long-term market yields imposes no constraint. The significance of the interrelationship between long and short rates actually runs in the opposite direction. It is the greater sensitivity of the long market to small changes in short-term rates that gives added impact to any change in short rates. Thus, while short rates can be permitted to vary over a rather wide range, they will probably not have to do so in the interest of an effective credit policy. Short-term rates can certainly fluctuate over a sufficient range to make uncertainty concerning possible changes in these rates a powerful tool of central bank control over the availability of credit.

IV. CONCLUSIONS

Central banking and interest rate control have passed through two extremes of public favor and disfavor during the past half-century, and now appear to be settling themselves somewhere in between. First they were seized upon as panaceas; then shunted aside in favor of another panacea, fiscal policy; and now they are being rediscovered, are recognized as more delicate and flexible than fiscal policy for early action against cyclical swings, and are accepted as one among a number of sets of influences that may be helpful in attempting to stabilize over-all economic activity. This paper has been concerned mainly with the changing theory and application of central bank control over interest rates through these three phases, with emphasis upon the scope of action that has ultimately emerged.

The growth of a large public debt, providing a medium for effective central bank influence upon the interest rate structure, has coincided with an increased channeling of investable resources into lending institutions which have, by their nature, a high sensitivity to small changes in yield among alternative debt instruments. Through its guidance of prices in the Government securities markets the central bank can, therefore, exert a powerful influence upon the volume and timing of changes in the general availability of credit. It is principally through effects upon the position and decisions of lenders, and only secondarily through effects upon the decisions of borrowers and savers, that central bank action affecting interest rates achieves its significance.

There are, of course, many aspects of these relatively recent developments which have been ignored by this paper in focusing attention upon the potentialities of central bank control. Treasury debt management, particularly the term distribution and the offering rates of the large annual volume of refinancing, pose related problems; so do the Treasury's current surpluses or deficits, arising from the Government's over-all fiscal policy. Conceivably, Treasury action could, for example, by shifting drastically the proportions of debt in long-term and short-term form, raise or lower the "permanent" level of yields on long-term securities which, for the present analysis, has been accepted as given. But whether the average level of long-term rates should eventually shift, or remain where it is, the major impact of central bank policies at any given time will be produced by the effects on the current prospects of lenders of changes in the availability of Federal Reserve credit, and the accompanying relatively small changes within the existing rate structure — primarily upward or downward changes in the rates on Government securities.

While still immediately concerned with the commercial banks, and bank reserves, the central bank has now been brought closer to other lenders. For virtually all lenders have a substantial proportion of Government securities in their portfolios, and the general availability of credit to the private sector of the economy is determined in large measure by the willingness and the ease with which lenders can shift into or out of Government securities, at the margin. Since the central bank, because of the immensity of the public debt, cannot avoid a controlling responsibility for the prices (and yields) of these securities, its influence at the critical margin of lenders' decisions is similarly unavoidable. If diverted solely to the rigid support of Government security prices, central bank action can be prevented from exerting any effective contra-cyclical control over the availability of credit — no device can be substituted for, or employed successfully to suppress, the inherent causal relationship between a guided variation in credit availability and variation in interest rates. Carefully exercised, through selective operations in the open market, central bank influence can effect a meaningful restraint upon, or inducement toward, the readiness of lenders to extend private credit.

As had been generally accepted in earlier periods, any central bank action in the modern setting is likely to be most powerful in restraining excessive credit expansion, somewhat less powerful in reversing a credit contraction during its early stages, and relatively weak in stimulating credit expansion in the more severe stages of cyclical depression. In any of these situations, the extent of the influence will depend upon early timing, and require the use of delicate (and readily reversible) instruments. But there is clearly a useful contribution to be made — through the creation of market uncertainty over rate movements, through a simple reversal in the direction of rate movements, and through small and successive rate changes in a consistent direction. The central bank can now reach directly into the short-term and the long-term money markets, serving through the impersonal mechanism of these markets as the arbiter of general credit availability.

PART TWO

THE SIGNIFICANCE OF GOVERNMENT DEBT AND FINANCIAL INTERMEDIARIES: TWO OPPOSING VIEWS

WARREN L. SMITH

Some Limitations on the Overall Effectiveness of Monetary Policy*

Warren L. Smith inquires: Have the size of the public debt and the increased importance of financial intermediaries—insurance companies, savings banks, savings-and-loan associations and others— reduced the effectiveness of monetary policy? His answer is in the affirmative. Focusing on the effectiveness of a policy of monetary restraint, he argues that commercial banks can at least partly offset the effects of tight money by selling some of their large holdings of government securities and using the proceeds to accommodate their borrowers. Simultaneously, financial intermediaries also sell government bonds, a policy which enables them to increase their loans, although the author finds this of less importance quantitatively than the case of commercial banks. It will be noted that this conclusion, which is based on evidence gained since the Federal Reserve-Treasury accord of 1951, differs from the expectation expressed by Rosa in 1951, that

* Reprinted from U. S. Congress Joint Economic Committee, *Staff Report on Employment Growth and Price Levels* (U. S. Government Printing Office, 1959), pp. 344–62.

financial institutions would be unwilling to sell government securities when their prices fell in response to a rise in interest rates. According to Smith, an additional factor is that with higher interest rates there is a shift from demand deposits into deposits at the interest-paying intermediaries. Because reserve requirements of the latter are very much lower than those for commercial banks, this, too, permits more lending. In all of these instances, the effect is to activate idle balances and increase velocity, thereby, in part or in whole, negating the attempt at monetary restriction. The supply of money may remain constant but its velocity increases, thus leading to an increase in spending. To support his general view, Smith demonstrates that the cyclical fluctuations from 1947 to 1959 have corresponded far more with changes in velocity than with changes in the money supply.

T HE United States possesses a highly complex and sophisticated financial system, including some 13,000 commercial banks and a myriad of other financial institutions. The variety, complexity, and sophistication of this system have increased greatly in recent years and can be expected to increase further in the years to come. In assessing the effectiveness of monetary controls in an economy possessing such a complex financial structure, it is important to bear in mind the simple fact that the basic function of financial institutions is the financing of economic activity and that the variety of channels through which such financing may be provided is very great. It is not surprising therefore to find that when credit conditions are tightened and the creation of new money through the banking system is restricted, pressures are automatically set up which cause the financial system to "hunt" for methods of mobilizing the existing money supply more effectively, thus permitting it to do part, or perhaps even most, of the work that would have been done by newly created money had credit conditions been easier.

The fact that there has been a considerable amount of "play" in our financial system is illustrated in table I, which shows the changes in money supply and income velocity during alternating periods of business expansion and contraction since the first quarter of 1947. In each upward or downward movement, the change in velocity has been a more important factor than the change in the money supply, and velocity has consistently tended to rise during periods of expansion and credit restriction and to fall during periods of contraction and monetary ease. The last row of the table shows approximations of the changes in the quantity of money that would have been necessary to produce effects on GNP expenditures equivalent to the changes in velocity that occurred during each period.

TABLE I — COMPARISON OF CHANGES IN MONEY SUPPLY AND IN INCOME VELOCITY DURING UPWARD AND DOWNWARD MOVEMENTS OF GROSS NATIONAL PRODUCT SINCE THE 1ST QUARTER OF 1947

	Year and quarter							
	1947 I	1948 IV	1949 IV	1953 II	1954 II	1957 III	1958 II	1959 II
GNP[1]	226.0	265.9	257.0	368.8	358.9	447.8	434.5	484.5
Money supply[2]	108.2	109.3	108.6	125.9	126.6	134.6	134.8	140.6
Income velocity[3]	2.09	2.43	2.37	2.93	2.84	3.33	3.22	3.45
Percent change in GNP		+17.7	−3.4	+43.5	−2.7	+24.8	−3.0	+11.5
Percent change in money supply		+1.0	−.7	+15.9	+.6	+6.3	+.1	+4.3
Percent change in velocity		+16.3	−2.5	+23.6	−3.1	+17.3	−3.3	+7.1
Absolute change in money supply (billions of dollars)		+1.1	−.7	+17.3	+.7	+8.0	+.2	+5.8
Approximate monetary equivalent of change in velocity (billions)[4]		+17.6	−2.7	+25.6	−3.9	+21.9	−4.4	+9.6

[1] Seasonally adjusted annual rate in billions of current dollars, Department of Commerce.

[2] Demand deposits adjusted plus currency outside banks in billions of dollars, seasonally adjusted, average for beginning and end of quarter. Board of Governors of the Federal Reserve System.

[3] GNP (row 1) divided by money supply (row 2).

[4] Estimated by multiplying the money supply for the previous period by the percentage change in velocity since that period (e.g., the $17,600,000,000 estimate for the period from the 1st quarter of 1947 to the 4th quarter of 1948 equals 108.2 × 0.163).

Some students of monetary matters have argued that the growth of the Government securities market and the increase in its efficiency, which have characterized the period since World War II, together with the increased importance of large financial institutions, have considerably strengthened the influence of the Federal Reserve by providing a sensitive medium which rapidly transmits the effects of its actions to all sectors of the economy. Moreover, large institutional investors are sensitive to small changes in interest rates and security prices, and it is said that the System can rely upon those sensitive reactions as a means of influencing the supply of funds these institutions are prepared to make available to the private sector of the economy.[1]

While there is probably some truth in these contentions, it appears that, on balance, the growth of the public debt, the increased efficiency of the Government securities market, and the expanded role of sophisticated financial institutions have reduced rather than increased the effectiveness of monetary policy. The existence of a large and widely held public debt traded in a highly efficient market has added greatly to the efficiency of the process of mobilizing existing funds in support of economic activity by providing a vehicle for the necessary transfers of funds among economic units. And the large financial institutions have proved to be exceedingly skilled and resourceful participants in this mobilization process. Let us consider some of the more important channels through which this process has worked in the last few years.

A. THE EFFECTS OF COMMERCIAL BANK PORTFOLIO ADJUSTMENTS

In our earlier discussion of the developments in monetary and debt management policy since 1946, the reader's attention was called on several occasions to shifts in the composition of bank portfolios from Government securities to loans in periods of credit restriction such as 1955–57 and to the building up of the Government security holdings of the banks in periods of easy money such as 1953–54 and 1957–58.[2] These adjustments in bank portfolios have been quite systematic in the last few years and appear to have weakened the overall effectiveness of monetary controls rather substantially. The facts are assembled systematically in table II, which shows the major factors affecting the publicly held money supply (demand deposits and currency) for alternating periods of monetary restriction and monetary

[1] See R. V. Rosa, "Interest Rates and the Central Bank," in Money, Trade, and Economic Growth: In Honor of John Henry Williams (New York, 1951); also Rosa's "Federal Reserve Operations in the Money and Government Securities Markets" (Federal Reserve Bank of New York, 1956).

[2] There was also a sizable shift from Government securities to loans in 1947–48, but in the present discussion we shall confine our attention to the period of rather vigorous monetary policy since late 1952.

TABLE II — FACTORS RESPONSIBLE FOR CHANGES IN MONEY SUPPLY
DURING PERIODS OF MONETARY EASE AND RESTRICTION,
NOV. 26, 1952, TO SEPT. 30, 1959

[Billions of dollars]

	Restriction, Nov. 26, 1952 to May 27, 1953	Ease, May 27, 1953 to Dec. 31, 1954	Restriction, Dec. 31, 1954 to Sept. 25, 1957	Ease, Sept. 25, 1957 to Nov. 26, 1958	Restriction, Nov. 26, 1958 to Sept. 30, 1959[1]
Expansive factors:					
Bank loans and private securities[2]	+2.8	+11.8	+29.0	+9.0	+13.8
Commercial banks[3]	+2.2	+7.1	+23.5	+5.9	+12.1
Mutual savings banks[3]	+1.1	+3.7	+6.5	+3.2	+1.7
Bank holdings of U.S. Government obligations	−5.8	+9.9	−14.0	+11.3	−8.5
Commercial banks	−5.8	+10.7	−13.1	+11.8	−8.5
Mutual savings banks	+.1	−.8	−.9	−.6	0
Total expansive factors	−3.0	+21.7	+15.0	+20.3	+5.3
Less: Contractive factors:					
Time deposits	+2.8	+7.7	+12.4	+9.1	+4.8
Commercial banks	+1.7	+5.1	+8.3	+7.0	+3.6
Mutual savings banks	+1.0	+2.5	+4.2	+2.0	+1.3
Other factors, net	−3.5	+4.1	+3.7	+3.8	+1.4
Total contractive factors	−.7	+11.8	+16.1	+12.9	+6.2
Equals: Change in money supply	−2.3	+9.9	−1.1	+7.4	−.9

[1] Preliminary.

[2] Including State and local government securities.

[3] The loan breakdown between commercial banks and mutual savings banks is on a different basis from the total for the banking system, so the components for some periods do not add to the total.

NOTE. — Details may not add to totals due to rounding.

Source: Federal Reserve Bulletin.

ease since late 1952.[3] The money supply has been reduced at least slightly in each period of restriction and has expanded substantially in each period of ease.[4] However, during the 1954–57 and 1958–59 periods of restriction, bank loans to the private sector and holdings of securities other than those of the Federal Government have continued

[3] The separation into periods of restriction and ease is based on an overall assessment of Federal Reserve policy. Doubtless, it would be possible to quarrel with the selection of dates, but reasonable changes in them do not affect the results significantly.

[4] It should be noted that the money supply figures in table II are not adjusted for seasonal variation; after such an adjustment is made, the money supply usually shows some increase even in periods of credit restriction.

to increase — in fact the rate of increase has accelerated substantially during such periods. The chief explanation for this is that banks have systematically added to their holdings of Government securities during periods when credit conditions have been easy and the supply of reserves has been large relative to private loan demands.[5] Then during periods of restriction, they have sold Government securities in the market or let them run off at maturity without replacement and used the funds to make loans.

Monetary policy is commonly admitted to be of no more than limited value in stimulating recovery from recession; moreover, to the extent that it can do any good, there is nothing to prevent the authorities from pressing their policies more vigorously if necessary to overcome the tendency of the banks to use the influx of reserves to buy Government securities instead of expanding their loans. Accordingly, the portfolio adjustments referred to above are chiefly a problem in connection with restrictive policy — as are the other offsets discussed below — and we shall concentrate most of our attention on monetary policy as an anti-inflationary weapon.

A few years ago there was much concern about the inflationary effects of monetization of public debt by the banking system. By analogy, it might seem at first glance that demonetization of debt — shifting it out of the banking system — during periods of inflation would be effectively anti-inflationary. Or, looking a little more carefully and observing that the bank sales of public debt during such periods have been accompanied by increases in loans to the private sector, thus leaving total bank earning assets and the money supply unchanged, one might conclude that such operations would be approximately neutral in their effects. However, even this view is almost certainly incorrect. Taken by themselves, sales of Government securities by the banking system to other investors could be expected to have some restrictive effects, since they reduce the money supply and push up interest rates. Loan expansion, on the other hand, is strongly inflationary, because it creates money which in most cases is promptly used to finance income-generating expenditures. The combined operation of liquidating securities and expanding loans will be inflationary on balance unless the security sales reduce income-generating expenditures as much as the loans increase them. To this extent, the active portion of the money supply is not increased — it is reduced by

[5] The other main factor explaining the rapid expansion of loans during periods of monetary restriction is the continued expansion of time deposits. This is discussed below.

the security sales and increased by the lending — and the total amount of spending is little affected, although its direction may be changed. However, it does not seem reasonable to expect such results. Due to the apparent insensitivity of expenditures to interest rate changes, it is likely that, in effect, the deposits extinguished by the security sales will be largely idle deposits. These deposits are then recreated through lending and promptly inserted directly into the spending stream. The net result of the operation is to leave the money supply unchanged but to increase the velocity of monetary circulation by expanding the fraction of the money supply that is being actively spent at the expense of the fraction that is being held idle.[6]

One of the arguments that has been stressed in connection with monetary policy in recent years is that the fall in security prices caused by a restrictive credit policy will induce banks and other financial institutions to hold onto Government securities in order to avoid realizing capital losses, instead of selling such securities and using the proceeds to make private loans or buy private securities. This is an important one of the means by which a small rise in interest rates is supposed to reduce the supply of funds available to finance private spending. Under some circumstances, there is probably something to this so-called locking-in argument. For example, if investors expect the rise in interest rates to be reversed shortly, they will recoup their initial capital loss if they hold onto the securities, and accordingly they may require a higher interest rate on loans to make up for it. However, unless there is something to prevent loan interest rates from rising or unless the demand for loans is sensitive to interest rates, this is not likely to be important. Moreover, if interest rates are expected to go on rising for some time — as is often likely to be the case in the early stages of a boom — the effect may be turned in reverse and lenders may be particularly eager to shift into loans. Of course, in some cases, there may be a somewhat irrational desire to avoid showing losses on the lender's books, which may impede somewhat the tendency to shift out of Government securities during periods of rising interest rates.

In any case, it is apparent from the record that commercial banks have been quite willing to shift the composition of their portfolios in a destabilizing fashion. Whatever the merits of the "locking-in" argument, it does not appear to have affected banks, one reason prob-

[6] For an elaboration of this argument, see W. L. Smith, "On the Effectiveness of Monetary Policy," *American Economic Review*, XLVI, September 1956, pp. 588–606, especially pp. 600–604.

ably being that banks normally hold large amounts of short-term securities whose prices fluctuate little and for which potential capital losses are therefore a relatively unimportant matter. In addition, the peculiar Federal tax provisions applicable to commercial banks, which permit them to deduct capital losses from ordinary income, while paying lower rates on capital gains, have the effect of encouraging frequent portfolio adjustments during periods of rising interest rates, since the tax savings on the capital losses exceed the tax liability on the capital gains which will accrue when security prices rise at a later time. These tax provisions do not provide any direct inducement to shift from Government securities to private debt, since the benefits can be obtained by reinvesting in Government securities similar to those sold (the wash sale rule prevents reinvesting in identical securities within 30 days of the sale). But the provisions undoubtedly encourage more frequent portfolio adjustments and thus indirectly promote shifting.[7]

Due mainly to the tremendous expansion of bank loans that has occurred in the last few years, Government security holdings of banks have been declining as a percentage of total loans and investments. In December 1952 Government security holdings of all commercial banks constituted 45 percent of their total loans and investments; by August 1959 this ratio had fallen to 32 percent. This suggests that the scope for destabilizing portfolio adjustments has been declining. However, the absolute amount of bank holdings of Government securities is now nearly as large as it was in 1952, and there does not seem to be any reason why the ratio cannot go much lower than it is now. Thus, while the bank portfolio adjustment mechanism may eventually tighten to the point where the importance of this loophole in monetary controls is greatly reduced, there is little reason to suppose that this problem will not be with us for some time to come. In support of this position, it may be noted that in the first 10 months (from the end of November 1958 to the end of September 1959) of the present period of credit restriction, the loan expansion of commercial and savings banks ($13.8 billion as shown in table II) has actually been larger than the expansion ($10.1 billion) in the first 10 months (from the end of December 1954 to the end of October 1955) of the corresponding period of 1955–57. Banks sales of Government securities have also been larger ($8.5 billion) than in the earlier period ($6.3 billion).

[7] For a good discussion of these tax provisions, see R. H. Parks, "Income and Tax Aspects of Commercial Bank Portfolio Operations in Treasury Securities," National Tax Journal, XI, March 1958, pp. 21–34.

B. ADJUSTMENTS IN CORPORATE LIQUIDITY

While not nearly as serious a problem as the commercial bank adjustments just discussed, the way in which nonfinancial business corporations have managed their liquid reserves in recent years appears to have facilitated the mobilization of funds during periods of tight credit and to have weakened the Federal Reserve's controls somewhat. There has been a noticeable tendency recently for large corporate treasurers to manage their cash balances more carefully and to keep their surplus funds invested in short-term Government securities, particularly at times when short-term interest rates have been high.[8] As a result, changes in corporate liquidity positions have been reflected mainly in changes in holdings of Government securities. These holdings are influenced by a number of variables, including interest rates, corporate profits, dividends, tax accruals, and investment in plant and equipment and inventories.

Despite the complexity of the factors involved, a fairly clear pattern seems to emerge on the basis of study of the last few years. From the second quarter of 1954 to the fourth quarter of 1955, corporate holdings of Government securities increased rather steadily from $16.4 billion to $24 billion, a rise of $7.6 billion. From the fourth quarter of 1955 to the second quarter of 1958 holdings declined, reaching $13.9 billion at the end of the period for a drop of $10.1 billion. At this point holdings began to rise again and by the second quarter of 1959 had reached $20 billion, $6.1 billion above the low point.[9] Thus, corporations have built up their holdings of Government securities in the early recovery periods (mid-1954 to the end of 1957 and mid-1958 to early 1959) and, at least in the 1956–58 period, reduced their holdings during the latter part of the expansion and during the decline. Table III, which is compiled from Federal Reserve flow-of-funds data covering the nonfinancial corporate sector, shows the sources and uses of corporate funds on a quarterly average

[8] See C. E. Silberman, "The Big Corporate Lenders," *Fortune*, August 1956, pp. 111–114, 162–170. On the theory of optimum cash balance management and the resulting interest elasticity of demand for transactions balances, see W. J. Baumol, "The Transactions Demand for Cash: An Inventory Theoretic Approach," *Quarterly Journal of Economics*, LXVI, November 1952, pp. 545–556, and James Tobin, "The Interest Elasticity of the Transactions Demand for Cash," *Review of Economics and Statistics*, XXXVIII, August 1956, pp. 241–247.

[9] These data are taken from the statements of current assets and liabilities of corporations as compiled by the Securities and Exchange Commission and published in the *Federal Reserve Bulletin*.

TABLE III — SOURCES AND USES OF FUNDS FOR NONFINANCIAL CORPORA-
TIONS BY SUBPERIODS, JUNE 30, 1954 TO MAR. 31, 1959

[Quarterly averages in billions of dollars]

	June 30, 1954, to Dec. 31, 1955	Dec. 31, 1955, to June 30, 1958	June 30, 1958, to Mar. 31, 1959
Excess of retained earnings and capital consumption allowances over investment in fixed capital and inventories	1.0	—1.9	2.0
Plus: Funds raised externally[1]	1.9	2.8	2.0
Less: Statistical discrepancy	.8	.5	1.2
Equals: Net acquisition of financial assets	2.1	.4	2.8
Federal obligations	1.2	—1.0	2.0
Currency and demand deposits	.7	—.2	.2
Trade credit[2]	—.1	1.0	.4
Other financial assets[3]	.3	.6	.3

[1] Funds raised by sale of corporate stocks and bonds and other forms of debt.
[2] Net trade credit extended by the nonfinancial corporate sector to other sectors. Borrowing and lending within the corporate sector is canceled out.
[3] Includes consumer credit, finance company paper, other miscellaneous financial assets, and time deposits.
Source: Federal Reserve Flow of Funds Accounts.

basis for the periods when corporations were accumulating and decumulating Government securities since mid-1954.[10]

During the early period of recovery from mid-1954 to the end of 1955, corporate profits and depreciation allowances were rising faster than investment in plant and equipment and inventories so that there was an excess of about $1 billion per quarter of funds from internal sources over the requirements for financing investment. In addition, funds were being raised from external sources at a rate of nearly $2 billion per quarter. These funds from internal and external sources were used chiefly to build up corporate liquidity, partly in the form of cash balances but to a greater extent by accumulating Government securities at a rate of $1.2 billion per quarter. From late 1955 to mid-1958, the situation was reversed, with real investment running nearly $2 billion a quarter ahead of funds becoming available from internal sources. In addition, corporations were extending net book credit to their noncorporate customers at a rate of $1 billion a quarter. To meet these needs, corporations speeded up sales of securities

[10] The data given in table III are not entirely consistent with the SEC estimates referred to above due to differences in sector coverage.

and borrowings to obtain funds from external sources at a rate of $2.8 billion a quarter and at the same time liquidated Government securities at a rate of $1 billion a quarter. From the time the upturn in business activity began in mid-1958 through March 1959, the situation was again reversed, with funds available from internal sources exceeding investment needs, fund-raising from external sources slowing down, and Government securities accumulating at a rate of $2 billion a quarter. It may be noted that in the last few years corporations have been investing some of their surplus funds in liquid short-term instruments other than Government securities, such as repurchase agreements with Government security dealers and commercial paper issued by sales finance companies, although these operations are still much less important quantitatively than investments in Government securities.[11]

This pattern of corporate financial activities, particularly with respect to investment and disinvestment in Government securities increases the mobility of funds and probably reduces somewhat the ease with which the Federal Reserve can bring pressure to bear on the financial system. In the early stages of credit restriction, the increased supply of funds becoming available through corporations reduces the pressure on the banking system somewhat, since corporations may either buy securities being sold by banks that are in the process of shifting from Government securities to loans or may take some customers off the hands of the banks by providing funds to Government security dealers and sales finance companies.[12] At a later stage in the process, corporations may sell off their holdings which are taken up by other investors (including the Government itself which is likely to be retiring debt) and using the funds to finance their own expenditures or to lend to customers thus enabling them to escape the effects of the credit squeeze. In other words, these Government securities transactions make it possible to tap successive pools of funds in various parts of the economy which in the absence of such transactions might have been held idle.

C. EFFECTS OF FINANCIAL INTERMEDIARIES ON VELOCITY

There has been much controversy recently concerning the effects on monetary policy of the rapid growth of financial intermediaries, such as mutual savings banks, savings and loan associations, insurance com-

---

[11] Silberman, op. cit.

[12] During the 1958–59 recovery, the expanding corporate holdings of Government securities also helped to provide a market for new short-term securities for the Treasury, which was borrowing heavily to finance a deficit.

panies, pension trusts, investment trusts, and the like. One school of thought has contended that the presence of such a large sector of the financial system outside the reach of Federal Reserve authority has seriously reduced the effectiveness of the traditional monetary controls.[13] Others have disagreed, arguing either that the destabilizing effects of intermediaries do not appear to have been very important or that they are influenced powerfully, albeit indirectly, by the Federal Reserve's actions.[14]

There can be little disagreement concerning the fact that, at least since the end of World War II, financial intermediaries have grown much more rapidly than commercial banks. For the period prior to 1952, this growth is amply documented in the recent study by Raymond Goldsmith.[15] The Federal Reserve flow-of-funds studies show clearly that since 1952 the disparity in rates of growth between commercial banks and intermediaries has continued. Perhaps the best indication of this is that between 1952 and 1957, demand deposits increased by 7 percent while outstanding intermediary claims (including time deposits of commercial banks, since the savings banking activities of these banks should be treated as intermediary operations) increased by 47 percent.[16]

One question which has been the subject of considerable discussion has been whether the ability to expand credit which commercial banks are agreed to possess is shared by other types of financial institutions such as mutual savings banks and savings and loan associations which issue claims (savings deposits and savings and loan shares) that are close substitutes for money (demand deposits and currency). Since nearly all of the savings deposits and shares are held by the

[13] Pioneering work on financial intermediaries reflecting this point of view has been done by J. G. Gurley and E. S. Shaw. See their articles, "Financial Aspects of Economic Development," American Economic Review, XLV, September 1955, pp. 515–538, and "Financial Intermediaries and the Saving-Investment Process," Journal of Finance, XI, May 1956, pp. 257–276.

[14] See for example, Joseph Ascheim, "Commercial Banks and Financial Intermediaries: Fallacies and Policy Implications," Journal of Political Economy, LXVII, February 1959, pp. 59–71; Donald Shelby, "Some Implications of the Growth of Financial Intermediaries," Journal of Finance, XIII, December 1958, pp. 527–541; G. W. McKinley, "The Federal Home Loan Bank System and the Control of Credit," Journal of Finance, XII, September 1957, pp. 319–332; W. L. Smith, "Financial Intermediaries and Monetary Controls," Quarterly Journal of Economics, LXXIII, November 1959, pp. 533–553.

[15] R. W. Goldsmith, "Financial Intermediaries in the American Economy Since 1900" (Princeton: Princeton University Press, 1958).

[16] These calculations are based on mimeographed tabulations obtained from the Board of Governors of the Federal Reserve System.

consumer sector and since most of the expansion of these claims appears to stem from bona fide saving out of current income, it appears that these institutions play a rather different economic role from that of commercial banks. To the extent that this is true, these institutions do not contribute to instability in aggregate spending, but merely serve to channel savings into investment, as their name implies. The expansion of commercial bank credit on the other hand is not linked directly with income growth but can proceed quickly and independently and therefore serve as a stimulant to income expansion. Moreover, commercial banks are not intermediaries since, when a part of income is saved and deposited in a commercial bank, no more funds are made available for investment than would have been provided if the income had been spent on consumption.[17]

If all the funds supplied to intermediaries were derived from current saving, as just pointed out, intermediaries would not be a destabilizing influence on aggregate demand — although, of course, they might cause trouble because of their effects on the allocation of credit and the composition of demand. However, intermediaries may at times play a role in the process of activating or deactivating cash balances thus causing velocity to rise or fall and contributing to instability. To take the case of inflationary increases in velocity attributable to intermediary activities, there seem to be two ways in which these might come about.

(1) When credit tightens and interest rates rise during inflationary periods, those intermediaries — such as savings banks and savings and loan associations — which issue claims that are close substitutes for money, may raise the interest rates or other incentives they offer to holders of their claims, the reason being that interest rates on the kinds of debt that intermediaries invest in are also increasing. To the extent that this induces members of the public to substitute intermediary claims for their holdings of demand deposits, the supply of credit is expanded, since reserve requirements applicable to intermediary claims are much smaller (in fact, virtually nonexistent in some cases) than reserve requirements applicable to demand deposits. When this happens, the intermediary, in effect, acts as an agent facilitating the process of dishoarding cash balances.

(2) Intermediaries may liquidate a portion of their holdings of securities — particularly Government securities — and use the proceeds

[17] See J. M. Culbertson, "Intermediaries and Monetary Theory: A Criticism of the Gurley-Shaw Theory," and J. G. Gurley and E. S. Shaw, "Reply," *American Economic Review*, XLVIII, March 1958, pp. 119–138; also Smith, "Financial Intermediaries and Monetary Controls," pp. 533–538.

for lending to the private sector. This is very similar to the process of shifting from Government securities to private loans on the part of commercial banks, which was explained at some length earlier in this chapter. To the extent that the securities are purchased by holders of idle cash balances and the proceeds of the new loans are spent on current output, the intermediary again serves as an agent to facilitate dishoarding, and the process is inflationary. More accurately, in fact, it can be said that there is an inflationary effect unless the rise in interest rates caused by the security sales results in a reduction in expenditures somewhere in the economy which is as large as the new expenditures financed out of the loan proceeds. An inflationary effect equal to a substantial proportion of such operations seems very likely.

If the reactions just discussed were sizable and systematically destabilizing, they could substantially weaken the monetary controls of the Federal Reserve. For example, if when the Federal Reserve strove to restrict credit, savings institutions quickly began to raise their interest rates and this caused a large shift of funds from commercial bank demand deposits to savings and loan shares and time deposits, the release of reserves thus brought about could substantially undercut the effects of the restrictive action. And if at the same time, intermediaries were induced to sell large quantities of Government securities which were, in effect, bought by holders of idle cash balances which were then activated by intermediary lending, monetary controls would be further weakened.

The question then is whether these reactions on the part of intermediaries are large and systematically destabilizing to a degree which poses a serious threat to the monetary authorities. The systematic destabilizing aspect is particularly important — that is, intermediaries will presumably be a serious problem only if the public systematically shifts funds from demand deposits to intermediary claims during periods of tight credit and then shifts back to demand deposits when credit eases and if intermediaries systematically sell Government securities in order to expand their loans when credit tightens and then rebuild their Government security portfolios when credit eases, as commercial banks have shown a tendency to do. If intermediaries merely grow more rapidly than banks, they represent part of a stable environment to which presumably the Federal Reserve should have no great difficulty in adapting itself.

Table IV shows the average amounts of credit extended to the private sector of the economy per quarter by intermediaries during alternating periods of credit restriction and credit ease between the end of 1952 and the end of 1958. The table indicates that the rate of credit extension by intermediaries speeded up noticeably during the

TABLE IV — SOURCES OF FUNDS SUPPLIED TO THE PRIVATE SECTOR BY
FINANCIAL INSTITUTIONS OTHER THAN COMMERCIAL BANKS
DURING PERIODS OF MONETARY EASE AND RESTRICTION,[1]
DEC. 31, 1952, TO DEC. 31, 1958

[Quarterly averages in billions of dollars]

	Restriction (Dec. 31, 1952 to June 30, 1953)	Ease (June 30, 1953 to Dec. 31, 1954)	Restriction (Dec. 31, 1954 to Sept. 30, 1957)	Ease (Sept. 30, 1957 to Dec. 31, 1958)
Total funds supplied to private sector[1][2]	4.2	4.3	4.9	4.6
Source of funds, total	4.2	4.3	4.9	4.6
Deposits in mutual savings banks	.5	.4	.4	.6
Savings shares[3]	1.0	1.1	1.3	1.6
Saving through life insurance	.7	.8	.8	.8
Saving through pension funds	.7	.7	.9	1.0
Issuance of credit and equity market instruments	.4	.5	.8	.5
Current surplus available for financial investment[4]	.6	.8	.6	.5
Sale of Federal obligations	[5]	.1	.2	—.2
Other sources, net, and statistical discrepancy	.2	—.2	[5]	—.2

[1] Includes mutual savings banks, savings and loan associations, credit unions, insurance companies (life and nonlife), private noninsurance pension, and retirement plans, sales finance companies, industrial and personal finance companies, mortgage companies, short-term business-finance companies, open-end investment companies, security and commodity exchange brokers and dealers, banks in U. S. territories and possessions, and agencies of foreign banks in the United States.

[2] Purchases of securities and other debt instruments of households, business firms, and state and local governments.

[3] Includes shares of savings and loan associations and credit unions.

[4] Includes premiums on life insurance and private pension plans, less benefit payments and policy dividends and less capital expenditures.

[5] Less than $50,000,000.

NOTE: Detail may not add to totals due to rounding.

Source: Federal Reserve flow-of-funds accounts.

1955–57 period of tight credit and then slowed down during the subsequent period of easier money. Part of the credit acceleration in the 1955–57 period was due to the increased rate of flow through savings and loan associations, but this acceleration continued after credit turned easier instead of reversing itself. Funds obtained through the issuance of credit and equity market instruments rose by about $300 million per quarter between 1953–54 and 1955–57 and declined by an equivalent amount in the ensuing period. Much of this movement is accounted for by changes in the rate at which sales finance companies issued commercial paper and other debt instruments to

obtain funds to finance consumer credit. These operations probably
contributed to the movements of velocity. For example, in 1955–57,
sales of finance company paper to investors — such as nonfinancial
corporations — who gave up cash balances which might otherwise have
been held idle or to banks, which sold more Government securities
than they otherwise would have in order to be able to buy the paper,
may have resulted indirectly in the dishoarding of cash balances and
contributed to the rise in velocity.[18] In addition, intermediaries
speeded up their sales of Government securities a little between 1953–
54 and 1955–57 and then actually became net buyers of such securities in 1957–58, and these portfolio adjustments, like those of commercial banks, probably had some destabilizing effects. It may be
noted that something over half the increase in the rate of flow of credit
through intermediaries between 1953–54 and 1955–57 can be accounted for by the rise in personal saving assuming that intermediaries
continued to obtain the same share of this saving. Thus, intermediaries contributed somewhat to instability in aggregate demand in this
period, but it appears that most of the funds they received were derived from current saving.

TABLE V — AVERAGE INTEREST RATES PAID ON VARIOUS TYPES OF
FIXED-VALUE REDEEMABLE CLAIMS, 1946–58

[Percent]

Year	Time deposits at commercial banks	Time deposits at mutual savings banks	Shares in savings and loan associations
1946	0.8	1.7	2.4
1947	.9	1.7	2.3
1948	.9	1.8	2.3
1949	.9	1.9	2.3
1950	.9	2.0	2.5
1951	1.1	2.1	2.6
1952	1.1	2.4	2.7
1953	1.1	2.5	2.8
1954	1.3	2.6	2.9
1955	1.4	2.7	2.9
1956	1.6	2.8	3.0
1957	2.1	3.0	3.3
1958	2.3	3.2	3.5

Source: Savings and Loan Fact Book, 1959.

[18] Sales finance companies differ considerably from most other intermediaries, since they sell few of their obligations directly to households, and much to
their intermediation is in the flow of bank credit rather than in the direct flow
of saving into investment (or consumption).

Perhaps one reason for the absence of systematic shifting between demand deposits and intermediary claims is the fact that, as indicated in table V, interest rates on time deposits and savings and loan shares have been rising steadily during the postwar period. When interest rates on other kinds of debt tend to fall, these interest rates continue to rise or at least fail to decline.

As pointed out above, insofar as their savings banking activities are concerned, commercial banks should be regarded as financial intermediaries. Shifts of funds from demand deposits to time deposits in commercial banks induced by higher interest rates on the latter would permit an expansion of credit, because the reserve requirements for time deposits are lower than for demand deposits. In this connection, there is some indication that in early 1957 when the Federal Reserve was applying a restrictive policy, a sharp rise in interest rates on time deposits in commercial banks did induce a noticeable shift of funds from demand deposits to commercial bank time deposits. This shift occurred shortly after the Federal Reserve and the Federal Deposit Insurance Corporation raised the maximum interest rates that could be paid on time deposits by member banks and insured nonmember banks from 2½ to 3 percent effective January 1, 1957.[19] It is interesting to note that the rapid accumulation of time deposits at commercial banks continued — in fact, even accelerated — in late 1957 and in 1958 after monetary policy had shifted in the direction of ease and interest rates in general were declining.

We may conclude that while activities of intermediaries do have some destabilizing effects, they do not seem to be as serious a problem in this regard as do portfolio adjustments by commercial banks.

D. CHANGES IN HOLDINGS OF TREASURY SECURITIES BY INVESTOR GROUPS

The above discussion has stressed the way in which investment and disinvestment in Treasury securities, particularly by commercial banks and nonfinancial corporations and perhaps also to some extent by financial intermediaries have tended to weaken monetary controls. In this connection, it would be helpful to know who it is that buys the securities when these investor groups sell. This is a matter that deserves much more attention than it has received, but with the presently available breakdown of ownership of Treasury securities, a detailed analysis is not possible. What little evidence can now be adduced is set forth in table VI, which shows the changes in holdings

[19] For a discussion of this episode, see Smith, "Financial Intermediaries and Monetary Controls," pp. 540–546.

of Treasury securities for the categories of investors included in the monthly Treasury Survey of Ownership during alternating periods of monetary restriction and ease during the period of actively flexible monetary policy since late 1952.[20]

TABLE VI — CHANGES IN HOLDINGS OF TREASURY SECURITIES DURING
PERIODS OF MONETARY EASE AND RESTRICTION,
NOV. 30, 1952, TO AUG. 31, 1959

[Amounts in billions; (+) represents an increase in holdings, (—) a decrease]

Investor group	Restriction, Nov. 30, 1952, to May 31, 1953	Ease, May 31, 1953, to Dec. 31, 1954	Restriction, Dec. 31, 1954, to Sept. 30, 1957	Ease, Sept. 30, 1957, to Nov. 30, 1958	Restriction, Nov. 30, 1958, to Aug. 31, 1959
U.S. Treasury[1]	+2.1	—9.4	+10.1	—9.3	—7.5
Federal Reserve	+.4	+.7	—1.6	+2.9	+.5
Commercial banks	—5.7	+10.7	—10.9	+9.7	—7.2
Mutual savings banks	+.1	—.8	—.9	—.6	(2)
Insurance companies	—.1	—1.0	—2.8	—.1	(2)
Nonfinancial corporations	+.8	—2.5	—3.6	+2.3	+5.6
State and local governments	+.8	+2.1	+3.4	(2)	+1.6
Individuals	+1.0	—1.0	+4.3	—5.0	+2.4
Miscellaneous investors[3]	+.6	+1.1	+2.0	+.0	+4.6

[1] (+) represents net retirement (purchases) and (—) net issuance (sales) of securities by the Treasury including the Treasury investment accounts.
[2] Less than $500 million.
[3] Includes savings and loan associations, dealers and brokers, foreign accounts, corporate pension funds and nonprofit institutions.

Source: Treasury Bulletin.

A few patterns are discernible in table VI. For one thing, it may be noted that individual investors have consistently been selling securities when commercial banks have been buying, and buying when commercial banks have been selling. Thus, shifts of securities between commercial banks and individual investors appear to have facilitated the destabilizing changes in commercial bank portfolios referred to above. Another and more important pattern that is apparent in every period but the last one is that the Treasury has been operating at surpluses and retiring debt when commercial banks have

[20] Changes in holdings of commercial banks as shown in table II do not agree with those shown in table VI. One reason is that the changes are shown at book value in table II and at face value in table VI. Another reason is that securities held in trust departments are included in table II, while they are not included in the "commercial banks" row (but are in the "individuals" row instead) in table VI.

beein unloading securities and has been operating at deficits and issuing securities when commercial banks have been investing in them. Thus, Treasury debt management has facilitated the shifting of commercial bank portfolios. State and local governments and miscellaneous investors have been steadily increasing their holdings of Treasury securities. In the miscellaneous investor group, the most important absorber of Government securities has been foreign accounts, while savings and loan associations and corporate pension funds have been increasing their holdings rather slowly.

Nonfinancial corporations do not show a consistent pattern in table VI for the reason that, as pointed out earlier, their behavior is out of phase in relation to the time periods used in this table. They tend to increase their holdings in the early stages of upswings in business activity and then begin to disinvest in the later stages of such periods.

E. OTHER OFFSETS TO MONETARY CONTROLS

In addition to the adjustments by commercial banks, nonfinancial corporations, and to some extent financial intermediaries just discussed, there are other ways in which cash balances can be economized and velocity increased when credit is tightened. One way, which is undoubtedly very important but difficult to measure, is through the direct expenditure of previously idle cash balances on goods and services by households, business units, and State and local governments.

A number of specialized financial arrangements for economizing cash balances either have been developed or have come to be more widely used in recent years as a consequence of restrictive credit policy. For example, there has been a notable increase in participation in the Federal funds market by banks; this has economized the use of reserves and permitted a given amount of reserves to support a larger supply of credit.[21] Sales finance companies have developed a

21 Although the Federal funds market has expanded considerably in the postwar as compared with the prewar period, it is still true that only a relatively small number of banks participate in it. For an extensive analysis, see Board of Governors of the Federal Reserve System, "The Federal Funds Market" (Washington, 1959). The argument that the increased use of the Federal funds market has economized reserves and increased velocity is developed in H. P. Minsky, "Central Banking and Money Market Changes," Quarterly Journal of Economics, LXXI, May 1957, pp. 171–187. The argument is actually a little dubious, since if banks did not use the Federal funds market as much as they do, they would probably borrow more from the Federal Reserve, thus increasing aggregate member bank reserves. If this is the case, the increased use of the Federal funds market may have strengthened rather than weakened monetary controls.

complex network for collecting funds, including credit lines with large numbers of banks and sales of commercial paper and debentures in the open market, which permit them to tap a considerable variety of lenders, and they have demonstrated great dexterity in shifting from one source to another in order to escape the effects of credit tightening.[22] Government security dealers have developed means, largely by the use of repurchase agreements, through which they can obtain funds from banks, business corporations, State and local governments, and other investors in all parts of the country in order to meet their constantly fluctuating needs for funds to finance their daily positions in Government securities.[23] State and local governments, like non-financial corporations, have become aware of the gains to be had from keeping their surplus funds more fully invested and have become much more active participants than formerly in the Government security and other financial markets. The recent participation of several thousand individual investors in a Treasury offering of a 5-percent note, in many cases apparently withdrawing funds from savings accounts to buy the securities, suggests that individual investors are becoming more sensitive to interest rates and interest rate differentials.[24] As a result of the increased participation of life insurance companies operating on a national scale as well as the easing of geographical restrictions on the investment of funds by savings and loan associations and the development of a secondary market for FHA-insured and VA-guaranteed mortgages, considerable progress has been made in broadening the market for mortgages and increasing the mobility of mortgage funds.

In these and many other ways, under the pressure of the restrictive monetary policies and rising interest rates that have prevailed much of the time in the last few years, the managers of our financial system, with the help of an increasingly sensitive investing public,

[22] On the fund-raising techniques used by sales finance companies, see the following sections of the Federal Reserve study, Consumer Installment Credit: "Consumer Installment Credit and the Credit Market," pt. I, vol 1, ch. 13; and E. Shapiro and D. Meiselman, "The Financing of Consumer Credit Institutions:" D. P. Jacobs, "Sources and Costs of Funds of Large Sales Finance Companies;" and J. S. Earley, "Comment," pt. II, vol 1, pp. 298–323, 324–413, and 414–423, respectively.

[23] Rosa, "Federal Reserve Operations in the Money and Government Securities Markets," (Federal Reserve Bank of New York, 1956), especially pp. 43–52.

[24] This 5-percent note, issued in October 1959 and maturing in August 1964 attracted 108,000 full-paid subscriptions for $25,000 or less, aggregating $941 million. For details, see Treasury Bulletin, October 1959, p. A–1.

have devised many ingenious methods of getting more financial mileage out of the existing supply of funds. Moreover, most changes of this kind, once wrought, become a permanent part of the financial system — we will certainly never return to the simpler and less sophisticated arrangements that formerly prevailed.[25] In fact, in future periods of credit restraint, these methods of economizing funds are likely to be used even more widely than in the past, and we can trust the ingenuity of our financial managers to uncover still further economizing techniques.

There is not much that can be done about this propensity of the financial system to be ingenious. It is a matter of numerous small adjustments, frequently quantitatively unimportant individually, but cumulatively constituting a significant "slippage" in our monetary controls. Moreover, it would probably be unwise to interfere with these developments even if it were possible to do so, since they have served to increase the mobility of funds, reduced interest rate differentials, and caused the market mechanism to perform more efficiently its basic function of allocating capital. Some reduction in the effectiveness of monetary controls is probably not too high a price to pay for these improvements, particularly in light of the other weaknesses of monetary policy to be taken up shortly.

F. WHY CAN'T INDUCED VELOCITY CHANGES BE OFFSET?

The above analysis has shown that when a restrictive monetary policy is applied through the use of general credit controls which reduce the supply of bank reserves, the decline in the supply of money relative to the demand for it tends to cause interest rates to rise, and this rise in interest rates triggers a series of adjustments, large and small, which result in more intensive use of the existing money supply and a rise in velocity. The obvious question is: Given the fact that there is a slippage through velocity, what is to prevent the monetary authorities from applying the controls with a sufficient intensity to compensate for the rise in velocity and thereby accomplish the desired objectives? There are several reasons why such an approach is not likely to be feasible.

[25] Minsky ("Central Banking and Money Market Changes") refers to developments of the sort we have been discussing as "institutional changes" which shift the relation between velocity and the interest rate, making it possible to have a higher velocity than formerly with the same interest rate.

1. Need to keep the financial markets on an even keel

It is almost certainly true, in principle at least, that it would be possible in given circumstances to produce any desired degree of restriction of *aggregate* monetary demand (within reason) by forcing interest rates high enough (with attendant tightening of the other dimensions of credit contracts). However, such evidence as we possess strongly suggests that aggregate spending is not very sensitive to changes in interest rates.[26] For this reason, even rather small destabilizing autonomous increases in aggregate demand might require very large increases in interest rates to restore equilibrium, and, as we have seen, the slippages in the monetary machinery mean that a large volume of central banking activity — e.g., open market sales of Government securities — is required to produce a given effect on interest rates.[27] Under these circumstances, if the monetary authorities attempt by relentless pressure to bring about changes in both money supply and interest rates of the necessary magnitude within a short period of time, they run the risk of extreme congestion in the long-term capital markets, widespread cancellation of investment plans, a collapse of expectations, and a sharp decline in business activity. On the other hand, a slow, cautious policy designed to avoid these dangers may take so long to arrive at its destination as to be, for all practical purposes, rather ineffective.

2. Debt management problems

In addition to its responsibility for the maintenance of a reasonable degree of general financial stability, the Federal Reserve has a special responsibility to the Treasury in connection with debt management. Except in a couple of instances, the Federal Reserve has not given direct support to the market at times of Treasury financing since late 1952,[28] but the System has had to relax the degree of its restriction at

[26] This matter is discussed at some length, on a sector-by-sector basis, in the next section of this chapter.

[27] In simple Keynesian terminology, we have a case in which the elasticity of liquidity preference is high and the elasticity of marginal efficiency of investment low, so that the link between the money supply and the level of expenditures is rather weak.

[28] In late November 1955, the Federal Reserve bought $167 million of 2⅝ percent 1-year certificates of indebtedness on a when-issued basis to help the Treasury over a rough spot that developed unexpectedly in connection with a large refunding operation. (Board of Governors of the Federal Reserve System, Annual Report, 1955, pp. 8, 109–110.) And at the time of the speculative episode in connection with the refunding of June 1958, the Federal Reserve again gave some support to the market, as indicated earlier.

times when the Treasury has been in the market with large refunding or cash borrowing operations in order to give the Treasury a chance to complete its financing successfully. When debt management operations are large and frequent and employ the techniques now in use, the Federal Reserve may have difficulty working in the restrictive policy which it feels is necessary between Treasury trips to the market. It might be possible to alleviate this problem somewhat by the development of more effective debt management techniques — a matter which is discussed later in this chapter — but realistically it seems likely that it cannot be eliminated entirely.

3. *Uncertainty*

A fact that is often overlooked but is a handicap to effective general monetary policy is that the authorities are seldom entirely certain what the near-term business outlook is. Even in periods when, in retrospect after all the facts are in, it is reasonably clear what the situation was, it is not necessarily true that at the time the outlook was clear to the authorities. A good example of this is to be found in 1956. In January of that year, the Federal Open Market Committee modified its policy, which had been directed chiefly at the prevention of inflation, to "take into account any deflationary tendencies in the economy." In the record of policy actions of the Open Market Committee, the explanation given for this action is that "the committee noted the currently reduced levels of farm prices and uncertainties in the housing and automobile markets; and it gave consideration to the view that the domestic economy after a year and a half of expansion might be nearing a cyclical peak and that a reaction might be in prospect before long."[29] Actually, as it turned out, the peak was not reached for another year and a half in mid–1957. The modified policy of "taking account of deflationary tendencies" was dropped at the March meeting of the committee but was restored in May as uncertainties reappeared on the horizon and remained in effect until August when it was again eliminated.[30] Later in the fall, the development of the crisis in the Middle East introduced a new element of uncertainty into the picture.

These considerations suggest that until we are able to forecast near-term economic developments with more confidence than is presently possible, monetary policy will necessarily contain an element of hesitancy and caution which is natural in the case of officials charged

[29] Board of Governors, Annual Report, 1956, pp. 19–20.
[30] Board of Governors, The Federal Reserve System, Annual Report, 1956, pp. 19–20.

with important responsibilities, uncertain as to exactly what kind of action the situation calls for, and concerned lest a mistake in policy might do serious harm to the economy.

4. Uneven incidence of monetary policy

Another reason why monetary policy must be applied cautiously is that while its aggregate effects may not be very strong, there are differential impacts on different parts of the economy. Thus, an anti-inflationary policy that is not strong enough to do very much good from an aggregative standpoint may have serious effects on certain sectors. The problems this raises are partly political; vigorous complaints are likely to be elicited from the sectors that are unduly affected. In addition, however, social values may be at stake — the sectors that are affected may in some cases be those where from the standpoint of broad social policy it is most important that expansion continue.

Apart from these problems, the differential sectoral impacts of general monetary policy, taken in conjunction with some of the fundamental features of the structure of the American economy that are emphasized elsewhere in this report, are sufficient to raise some new and hitherto unexplored questions concerning the effectiveness of general monetary controls, particularly as a means of controlling inflation. These problems have little to do with the slippages in the monetary mechanism that were emphasized above but would be present even if general controls worked with much more precision than they do at the present time so that there was a reasonably close relation between the money supply and the *aggregate* level of expenditures. The basic question is whether, given the selective effects of general monetary controls and given the nature of the present-day inflationary process, such controls can deal effectively with the problem of inflation without creating severe unemployment and seriously slowing down the rate of economic growth.

SUMMARY OF LIMITATIONS ON OVERALL EFFECTIVENESS OF MONETARY POLICY

With a complex financial system such as ours, when the monetary authorities change the money supply, a number of reactions tend to occur which weaken the effects of the action on aggregate demand by inducing changes in holdings of idle cash balances and corresponding changes in monetary velocity. This tendency is especially troublesome in the case of restrictive policy designed to deal with inflation. Some of the major offsetting adjustments are as follows.

(1) Commercial banks tend to shift the composition of their portfolios systematically from Government securities to loans when credit tightens and from loans to Government securities when credit eases. A shift from Government securities to loans absorbs idle cash balances from the public and releases them into the spending stream, while a shift from loans to Government securities has the opposite effect.

(2) Nonfinancial corporations have become important investors in Government securities, and they tend to build up their holdings of such securities in certain stages of the business cycle and to reduce them in other stages. Their actions appear to increase the flexibility of financial adjustments, thus weakening the impact of monetary policy.

(3) The normal activities of financial intermediaries (such as life insurance companies, savings banks, etc.) serve merely to channel saving into investment and are not destabilizing in their effects on aggregate spending, although they may have troublesome effects on the composition of expenditures. To the extent that there are systematic shifts between demand deposits and claims against intermediaries or systematic shifts in the composition of intermediaries' portfolios, these institutions may facilitate destabilizing changes in the velocity of money. While these effects are present, available evidence suggests that they are less important than adjustments by commercial banks.

(4) A number of changes in financial practice have been introduced in recent years, especially during periods of tight credit, which have improved the efficiency of the financial system and increased its resistance to Federal Reserve influence.

(5) The increased flexibility of the financial system has weakened the effectiveness of the Federal Reserve, particularly in dealing with inflation. It is difficult for the System to increase the scope and speed of its actions to compensate for offsetting reactions, because it runs the risk of upsetting financial markets and of interfering unduly with the Treasury's debt management activities and because uncertainty about the business outlook frequently requires it to proceed cautiously. And finally the unevenness of the effects of monetary policy on different sectors of the economy (*a*) makes it difficult to proceed vigorously for fear of an undue impact on sensitive sectors, and (*b*) in light of the structure of the economy and the nature of present-day problems, renders exclusive reliance on general monetary controls an unsatisfactory way of achieving sound stabilization objectives.

JOSEPH ASCHEIM

The Contrast between Commercial Banks
and Financial Intermediaries*

Ascheim takes issue with Smith and those economists who claim that the existence of a large public debt and the rise of financial intermediaries have led to a reduction in the effectiveness of monetary policy. (1) He disputes the alleged severity of the decline in relative importance of commercial banks. Rather, he finds that, if government financial institutions are excluded, the share of commercial bank assets in relation to those of all private financial institutions fell from 52.8 percent in 1900 to 41.4 percent in 1929 and stood at 44.5 percent in 1952. The rise from 1929 to 1952 was kept down due to the fact that since 1929 the rise in volume of time deposits of commercial banks has not kept pace with the increase in demand deposits. (2) The author suggests that the existence of a large and widely-held public debt has increased the interdependence of all financial institutions, in that central bank open-market operations affect the assets of financial intermediaries as well as commercial banks. The Federal Reserve thus has an important impact on the lending policies of all financial institutions. This is a view which was found also in the earlier selection by Rosa. (3) On the important point raised by Smith—that a policy of preventing or limiting a rise in the money supply can be offset by an increase in velocity—Ascheim points out that the central bank can restrict the money supply to whatever extent is necessary to counterbalance the effects of any change in velocity.

* From Joseph Ascheim, *Techniques of Monetary Control* (Baltimore. 1961), pp. 111–32. Abridged and reprinted by permission of the Johns Hopkins Press.

I. THE NEW APPROACH

In recent years, the economic role of commercial banks has become the object of widespread interest and concern in the wake of a new "theory of finance that encompasses the theory of money." In the course of development of this theory, its authors[1] have reached some far-reaching empirical, theoretical, and policy views that merit scrutiny and appraisal. Empirically, and with reference to the United States, it is averred that commercial banks have declined in economic importance relative to other financial institutions[2] since the turn of the century. Theoretically, and presumably with reference to every monetary system, it is argued that the conventional dichotomy between commercial banks, as creators of loanable funds, and financial intermediaries, as brokers of loanable funds, is fallacious. Finally, with regard to policy measures, it is suggested that the institutional limitation of direct central-bank control to commercial banks is too narrow. . . .

[1] John G. Gurley and Edward S. Shaw, "Financial Aspects of Economic Development," *American Economic Review*, xlv (September 1955), 515–538; Gurley and Shaw, "Financial Intermediaries and the Saving-Investment Process," *Journal of Finance*, xi (May 1956), 257–276; Gurley and Shaw, *Money in a Theory of Finance* (Washington, D. C.: The Brookings Institution, 1960). For discussion by others, see Warren L. Smith, "On the Effectiveness of Monetary Policy," *American Economic Review*, xlvi (September 1956), 600–606; S. Clark Beise, "Are Our Monetary Controls Outmoded?" *Vital Speeches*, xxiii (December 1956), 154–157; Donald K. David, *Announcement of a National Commission on Money and Credit* (New York: Committee for Economic Development, November 21, 1957), pp. 9–10; Arthur F. Burns, *Prosperity Without Inflation* (New York: Fordham University Press, 1957), pp. 43–65, 81–82; "An Overdue Study" (editorial), *New York Times*, November 25, 1956, p. E8; John M. Culbertson, "Intermediaries and Monetary Theory: A Criticism of the Gurley-Shaw Theory," *American Economic Review*, xlviii (March 1958), 119–31 (followed by Gurley and Shaw's "Reply," *ibid.*, pp. 132–138); James W. Angell, "The Monetary Standard: Objectives and Limitations," *American Economic Review*, xlviii (May 1958), 76–87 (and "Discussion" by Gurley, *ibid.*, pp. 103–105); United States Congress, Senate Committee on Finance, *Investigation of the Financial Condition of the United States: Compendium*, 85th Congress, 2nd Session (Washington, D. C.: U. S. Government Printing Office, 1958), pp. 56–63, 74, 77–79, 136, 169, 177–178, 315; Warren L. Smith, "Financial Intermediaries and Monetary Controls," *Quarterly Journal of Economics*, lxxiii (November 1959), 533–553.

[2] The term "financial institutions" is used to cover all enterprises, private and public, whose assets are predominantly claims and equities: banks of all kinds, savings and loan associations, credit unions, insurance companies, corporate pension funds, dealers and brokers, finance companies, government lending institutions, and others.

II. EMPIRICAL FINDINGS

The finding that commercial banks have declined in economic importance since 1900 relative to other financial institutions is a principal result of the pioneering study of Raymond W. Goldsmith, *Financial Intermediaries in the American Economy since 1900.*[3] Goldsmith finds that the share of commercial banks in the assets of all financial institutions declined from somewhat over one-half in 1900 to about one-third in 1952.[4]

1. The relative share of commercial banks

One qualification of this result is expressed by Goldsmith himself. He notes that "the decline for commercial banks leveled off in the early thirties, and that after a temporary increase apparently due to the credit inflation of World War II, and comparable decrease afterward, their share by 1952 had not fallen below its 1933 level."[5] That is, as Table I indicates, the share of commercial banks in the assets of all financial institutions was virtually the same in 1952 as in 1933 — about one-third.

A second qualification emerges from further examination of the data for financial institutions other than commercial banks also presented in Table I. In 1900, financial institutions were almost entirely private.[6] By 1952, financial institutions had come to include such sizable governmental agencies as the Federal Reserve System; Government pension, retirement, and social security funds; and Government lending institutions. In principle, the Government can grow as a financial institution (or group of institutions) by its own decree, whereas private financial institutions cannot. Furthermore, Government regulation of the policies of Government financial institutions poses a distinctly different type of problem than Government regulation of private financial institutions. Thus, from the viewpoint of both economic analysis and economic policy, the growth of commercial banks in relation to private financial institutions only, is at least

---

[3] A preliminary and abbreviated version of the results of this monograph appeared in Raymond W. Goldsmith, *The Share of Financial Intermediaries in National Wealth and National Assets, 1900–1949,* National Bureau of Economic Research Occasional Paper 42 (New York: 1954).

[4] Raymond W. Goldsmith, *Financial Intermediaries in the American Economy since 1900* (Princeton, New Jersey: Princeton University Press, 1958), pp. 4, 59, 75.

[5] *Ibid.,* p. 85.

[6] *Ibid.,* p. 79.

TABLE I — TOTAL ASSETS OF COMMERCIAL BANKS AND OF GOVERNMENT
FINANCIAL INSTITUTIONS AS RELATIVE SHARES

Year	Commercial-bank assets as per cent of assets of all financial institutions (1)	Assets of government financial institutions as per cent of assets of all financial institutions (2)	Commercial-bank assets as per cent of assets of private financial institutions (3)
1900	52.8	0.0	52.8
1912	53.5	0.2	53.6
1922	48.2	6.4	51.6
1929	39.6	4.5	41.4
1933	33.5	10.2	37.3
1939	32.7	17.9	39.9
1945	39.5	26.2	53.5
1949	34.9	24.7	46.3
1952	33.9	23.9	44.5

Sources: Raymond W. Goldsmith, *Financial Intermediaries in the American Economy since 1900* (Princeton, New Jersey: Princeton University Press, 1958), p. 75 for column (1) and p. 85 for column (2); column (3) was computed from pp. 73 and 85.

as relevant as the growth of commercial banks in relation to all financial institutions. Segregating, then, assets of Government agencies from those of private financial institutions, we find that the share of commercial banks in the assets of private financial institutions declined from 52.8 per cent in 1900 to 44.5 in 1952 — a much smaller decline than that of the share of commercial banks in the assets of private and public financial institutions combined.

As a third qualification, it should be noted that the share of commercial banks in the assets of all private financial institutions in 1952 was no lower (indeed, somewhat higher) than in 1929. Thus the decline of commercial banks relative to other private financial institutions was accomplished by 1929. Hence, alarm or concern over the relative decline of commercial banks is nearly a generation overdue, if any alarm or concern is called for.

2. *Relative shares within commercial-bank deposits*

Another aspect of the differential growth of commercial banks and of other financial institutions has not only been overlooked but covered up in the recent interpretations. As an almost inevitable result of the emphasis on the pathbreaking deviation "from conventional doctrine in regarding the banking system as one among many financial intermediaries,"[7] it has been ignored by the authors of the new

[7] Gurley and Shaw, "Financial Aspects of Economic Development," p. 521.

approach that American commercial banking consists of two distinct types of depository operations; demand-deposit operations (or commercial banking proper) and time-deposit operations (or savings banking). In their demand-deposit operations commercial banks create money, because demand deposits circulate as a widely accepted means of payment. In their time-deposit operations commercial banks do not create money, because time deposits do not circulate as a means of payment.

Table II shows the growth of both types of deposits for all operating commercial banks. In 1900 the ratio of time to demand deposits was 18.4 per cent; by 1952 this ratio had risen to 36.1 per cent. Thus over the period 1900–1952 as a whole, time deposits in commercial banks grew substantially more rapidly than demand deposits. But from 1929 (when the ratio of time deposits to demand deposits was at the high level of 75.8 per cent) to 1952, time deposits slightly more than doubled, whereas demand deposits grew substantially more than fourfold. In other words, since 1929 the growth of time deposits in commercial banks has lagged behind that of demand deposits. Indeed, had the growth of time deposits since 1929 kept pace with that of demand deposits, time deposits in commercial banks would have been higher by $47.5 billion in 1952 than they actually were. A corresponding addition of $47.5 billion to the assets of commercial banks by 1952 would have raised the share of commercial-bank assets to 55.8 per cent of the assets of all private financial institutions — a higher share than in 1900! Thus the smallness of the over-

TABLE II — DEPOSITS AT OPERATING COMMERCIAL BANKS

[In millions of dollars]

Year	Total deposits (1)	Demand deposits (2)	Time deposits (3)	Ratio of time to demand deposits (per cent) (4)
1900	6,812	5,752	1,060	18.4
1912	16,000	11,201	4,799	42.8
1922	34,300	21,822	12,478	57.2
1929	44,817	25,487	19,330	75.8
1933	30,930	18,997	11,933	62.8
1939	54,524	39,213	15,311	39.0
1945	140,517	110,205	30,312	27.5
1949	133,810	97,159	36,651	37.7
1952	157,301	115,542	41,759	36.1

Sources: Goldsmith, *Financial Intermediaries in the American Economy since 1900*, Table A-3.c.

all growth of commercial banks relative to other private financial institutions since 1929 is due to the relative decline of their time-deposit business. And it is in this type of business that commercial banks are akin to other financial institutions. . . .

III. POLICY IMPLICATIONS

The undiscriminating claims of a decline in the relative importance of commercial banks, coupled with the concurrent interpretation of monetary controls as being confined to commercial banks, has led to drastic policy conclusions. These have elicited favorable attention in academic,[8] commercial banking,[9] and public circles.[10]

The first conclusion is that the influence of general monetary policy, as formulated and carried out by the central bank, has been seriously weakened by the relative growth of financial institutions that have remained free from controls imposed on commercial banks.[11] The second conclusion is a corollary of the first: because the effectiveness of general monetary policy has been substantially curtailed by its being confined to commercial banks, the time has come to institute new controls that will encompass the operations of other financial enterprises.[12] The third conclusion, less frequently stated than the first two, is that the continued restriction of central-bank regulation to commercial banks may weaken the ability of commercial banks to attract enough capital to contribute significantly to the risky ventures of future economic growth.[13] It will be useful to examine the first two conclusions jointly and thereafter to turn to the third.

1. Control of financial intermediaries

The view that the influence of the monetary authority has been reduced by the relative growth of financial institutions other than commercial banks has two aspects: one is long-term or secular, the other is short-term or cyclical. The long-term aspect is that the rapid

[8] See, for example, Angell, *op cit.*
[9] See Beise, *op. cit.,* and his comments in *Investigation of the Financial Condition of the United States,* pp. 168–69; and J. S. Rockefeller's comments in the latter volume, *ibid.,* p. 315. Mr. Beise and Mr. Rockefeller are the presidents, respectively, of the Bank of America and the First National City Bank of New York, two of the three largest commercial banks in the United States.
[10] See "An Overdue Study," *New York Times,* November 25, 1956, p. E8.
[11] See references to Gurley and Shaw and to Smith in n. 1, this chapter.
[12] *Ibid.*
[13] Gurley's "Discussion," p. 105.

growth of nonbank financial institutions in the course of economic development implies that money (currency outside of banks and demand deposits) becomes a smaller proportion of total financial assets. In the long run, therefore, the velocity of circulation of money is higher than it would be without the rapid growth of nonbank financial institutions. Alternatively stated, the behavior of national income is not an adequate criterion for secular monetary expansion; the diversification demand for all types of financial assets must also be taken into account: "So short-term public debt may displace money, and debt management may displace monetary controls."[14]

One can accept the thesis that the rapid growth of nonbank financial institutions makes the velocity of circulation of money higher than it would otherwise be without inferring from this thesis that the influence of the monetary authority has declined. That the shaping of long-term monetary policy becomes increasingly complex in the course of economic development does not mean that the importance of monetary policy has to that extent diminished. On the contrary, the growing need to co-ordinate long-term monetary policy with considerations of fiscal policy and debt management adds to, rather than detracts from, the importance of a monetary policy consistent with, or conducive to, economic development.

Actually, it is the short-term or cyclical aspect of the alleged decline in the effectiveness of monetary policy that has received most of the attention in recent discussion. This is readily understandable, since the argument presented in this connection relates primarily to restrictive policy, and since it is largely as an anti-inflationary force that the potency of contra-cyclical monetary policy has been generally acknowledged. In other words, what has been commonly regarded as the most effective application of contra-cyclical monetary policy is now being challenged.[15]

The argument may be summarized as follows. The central bank controls the quantity of money by regulating the volume of reserves available to commercial banks. When aggregate monetary demand threatens to become excessive, the central bank can restrict the supply of reserves. In response to their tightened reserve position, commercial banks raise credit standards for borrowers and increase interest rates on loans. Now, if commercial banks were the only source of credit available to borrowers, the restrictive monetary policy would be quite effective. However, since credit can also be obtained from other

[14] Gurley and Shaw, "Financial Aspects of Economic Development," p. 535.
[15] See, in particular, Smith, "On the Effectiveness of Monetary Policy."

financial institutions, whose operations are not subject to quantitative control by the central bank, the efficacy of restrictive monetary policy is seriously reduced.

Further support for this argument is drawn from the existence of a large and widely distributed Government debt together with a broad and efficient market for Government securities. It is suggested that, as private demand for credit increases, financial institutions are both willing and able to liquidate their holdings of Government securities and to shift into loans. Indeed, it has been observed that even in the case of commercial banks the capacity and incentive to liquidate holdings of Government securities make it possible for them to expand loans in the face of their tightened reserve position.[16] This, as well as the similar capacity of other financial enterprises, is regarded as a large-scale sabotage of conventional monetary policy — a sabotage by means of an increased velocity of circulation of the unexpanded supply of money. The remedy for this state of affairs is held to be direct control of velocity through quantitative regulation of other financial institutions as well as of commercial banks.

So stated, the argument calls for immediate qualification.[17] If the Government securities sold by financial institutions are purchased by spending units that reduce their current expenditures in order to acquire the securities, the inflationary effect of increased loans by financial institutions would be counteracted by the deflationary effect of reduced current expenditures by buyers of Government securities. But since it seems more likely that holdings of idle balances, rather than current expenditures, will initially be reduced through the purchase of securities by spending units, this need not be a major qualification.

Another consideration, however, is of much broader significance. The large size and wide distribution of Government debt — which have given rise to the fear that restrictive monetary policy is undermined by compensating increases in velocity — augment the direct influence of the central bank on financial enterprises in general. Without growth in Government debt, conventional monetary policy is largely limited to variation of reserve requirements, rediscounting policy, and moral suasion, all of which are directly applied to commercial banks only. But with the expansion of the Government securities market to the point where it involves the great bulk of financial institutions, and with the growth of the securities portfolio

[16] *Ibid.,* p. 597.
[17] This is recognized by Smith (*ibid.,* p. 601).

of the central bank in relation to the reserve base of the money supply, open-market operations have a direct impact on the lending and investment activities of financial enterprises in general. Thus the growth in Government debt has widened the scope of direct contact between the monetary authority and the various financial institutions. It has heightened the interdependence between the various sectors of the money and capital markets, and has increased the substitutability between financial assets. In consequence, the direct effects of monetary policy on financial institutions of all types have been strengthened rather than weakened.

We now turn to the general proposition that the potency of conventionally restrictive monetary policy is seriously impaired by increases in velocity, permitting the currently restricted money supply to do much of the task that would have been performed by newly created money under an easier reserve position of commercial banks. The prime objective of restrictive monetary policy is to avert or check excess aggregate monetary demand; that is, to influence the volume of money expenditures so as to avert or arrest inflation. In principle, the volume of money expenditures can be influenced by controlling the quantity of money or its velocity or both. Any inflationary rise in velocity can be offset by a further restriction of the quantity of money. So long as the central bank has sufficient powers and resources to curtail the money supply, it will be able to offset any likely inflationary increases in velocity by correspondingly tightening commercial-bank reserves.

It may be suggested that the policy of offsetting increases in velocity is too dangerous, because it may precipitate a sharp break in business expectations with a resultant drop in aggregate business activity.[18] But this suggestion is hardly satisfactory as a basis for rejecting the policy of "offsetting." For the alternative approach would be the adoption of measures for the direct regulation of velocity. Rejection of the policy of offsetting would be warranted if it were shown that measures for the direct regulation of velocity were not only feasible but also free of the menace to business expectations which the policy of "offsetting" may entail. As the real world is riddled with "imperfections," it is not enough to demonstrate that existing monetary controls are imperfect. Before other measures are espoused, it must be shown that the present methods of control cannot be used more skillfully than they have been used in the past or that their more skillful application would be inferior to an alternative set of controls.

[18] Cf. Smith, *ibid.*, pp. 599–600; and Angell, *op. cit.*, p. 81.

PART THREE

RULES VERSUS DISCRETION:
THE FRIEDMAN THESIS

MILTON FRIEDMAN

The Goals and Criteria
of Monetary Policy*

In the following selection, Professor Friedman presents his well-known plea for the adoption of a system of rules versus discretion in monetary policy. First, he suggests this approach as a supporter of liberalism, opposed to the granting of too much power to any one institution such as the Federal Reserve or any other. Further, he contends that since its inception, the Federal Reserve has done a poor job of using its discretion and has succeeded in aggravating rather than mitigating economic instability. He argues that this is partly due to the fact that discretionary monetary policy leads to uncertainty, which is unsettling for businessmen. Also, he claims, on the basis of empirical investigation, that changes in the money supply have important effects on the economy but only after a long lag averaging sixteen months at the peak and twelve months at the troughs of eighteen business cycles. If such a long lag in fact exists, it necessitates basing monetary policy on anticipated economic conditions many months, and sometimes even years, in advance and it is most unlikely that our forecasting abilities

* Abridged and reprinted with permission from *A Program for Monetary Stability* by Milton Friedman (Fordham University Press, 1960), pp. 84–99.

87

are up to this difficult assignment. The issue, though, is whether the author's evidence on the length of the lag is accurate, and this has been seriously questioned, as will be seen in a later selection by Kareken and Solow. Following his reasons for objecting to the use of discretionary monetary policy, Friedman recommends what he considers an appropriate rule to guide the monetary authorities: *that the stock of money be increased at a regular rate year by year and month by month in accordance with the average secular growth of aggregate economic output.* With allowance for a secular decline in velocity, the figure he arrives at is approximately a 4 percent annual increase in the money supply. On the basis of his statistical tests, Friedman concludes that if such a rule had been in force since the beginning of the Federal Reserve System, there would have been far less economic instability than has in fact occurred. According to the author, this is especially true for the inter-war period, but he argues, with somewhat less conviction, that the same conclusion holds for the post-World War II period.

$\mathbf{G}$IVEN that we are not and should not be prepared to permit internal monetary policy to be dominated by either gold flows or other manifestations of foreign payment arrangements, there remains the central question: what is to be our internal monetary policy?

In a celebrated article on "Rules versus Authorities in Monetary Policy," Henry Simons contrasted sharply two ways of answering this question: one, by specifying a general goal and then giving monetary authorities wide powers to use at their discretion in promoting it; the other, by assigning specific responsibilities to monetary authorities to be carried out in accordance with rules specified in advance and known to all. As Simons made clear, the contrast is not complete. The general goal alone limits somewhat the discretion of the authorities and the powers assigned to them do so to an even greater extent; and reasonable rules are hardly capable of being written that do not leave some measure of discretion. Yet the contrast is nonetheless both marked and important.

In practice, we have relied almost wholly on authorities. . . . We have done so not by intention but because the change in the role of the gold standard brought about by World War I loosened so greatly what the authors of the Federal Reserve Act had expected to be the effective "rule" limiting the discretion of the monetary authorities. In the absence of the strait-jacket of a rigid gold standard, "accommodating commerce and business," to quote the original Federal Reserve Act, imposed hardly any restrictions on the discretion of the authorities.

Relying so largely on the discretion of authorities in so important an area of policy is highly objectionable on political grounds in a free society. Experience has demonstrated that it has also had unfortunate monetary consequences. It has meant continual and unpredictable shifts in the immediate guides to policy and in the content of policy as the persons and attitudes dominating the authorities have changed — from the "real bills" emphasis of the early 1920's to the offsetting of inventory speculation of the mid-20's to the restraint of stock market speculation of the late '20's to the sensitivity to external pressures and timidity in face of internal drains of the early '30's, to the bond-support policies of the '40's, to the sensitivity to cyclical movements and reliance on "announcement effects" of the '50's. It has meant continual exposure of the authorities to political and economic pressures and to the deceptive effects of short-lived tides of events and opinions. The role of the monetary authorities is to provide a stable monetary background, to go counter to or at least not reinforce the ever shifting tides of current opinion and events. This is the justification for their alleged "independence." Yet the vagueness of their responsibilities and the wide range of their discretion has left them no means other than "wisdom" and personal perspective of withstanding contemporaneous pressures and has denied them the bulwark that clearly assigned responsibilities and definite rules would have provided.

Reliance on discretion in pursuing general goals has meant also the absence of any satisfactory criteria for judging performance. This has made it nearly impossible to assess responsibility for success or failure and has greatly enhanced the difficulty of learning by experience. The Reserve System, or even monetary authorities more broadly defined, have not been the sole agencies responsible for the general goals that they have sought to promote, and that have become the current translation of "sound credit conditions and the accommodation of commerce, industry, and agriculture" — such general goals as economic stability, full employment, price stability, growth. These goals are to be approached through the joint actions of many public and private agencies, of which monetary authorities are only one. Success or failure in achieving them cannot be attributed to monetary policy alone, and hence cannot be a criterion of performance. An amusing dividend from reading *Annual Reports* of the Federal Reserve System *seriatim* is the sharp cyclical pattern that emerges in the potency attributed to monetary forces and policy. In years of prosperity, monetary policy is a potent instrument, the skillful handling of which deserves credit for the favorable course of events; in years of adversity, other forces are the important sources of economic change, monetary policy has little leeway, and only the skillful handling of the exceedingly limited powers available prevented conditions from being even worse.

The granting of wide and important responsibilities that are neither limited by clearly defined rules for guiding policy nor subject to test by external criteria of performance is a serious defect of our present monetary arrangements. It renders monetary policy a potential source of uncertainty and instability. It also gives greater power to the men in charge for good or ill, greater "flexibility" to meet problems as they arise, to use the phrase that the Reserve System likes to emphasize. . . . Experience suggests that eliminating the danger of instability and uncertainty of policy is far more urgent than preserving "flexibility." The major need in reforming our present control of monetary policy is, therefore, to provide more definite guides to policy and more satisfactory criteria of performance.

One way to do so that has frequently been urged is to adopt price level stability as simultaneously the specific goal for monetary policy, the immediate guide to policy, and the criterion of performance. There is much to recommend price level stability as the specific goal of monetary policy, as the way to separate the special role of monetary policy from that of other segments of economic policy in furthering our more nearly ultimate goals. The stock of money has a critical influence on the price level. No *substantial* movements in the price level within fairly short periods have occurred without movements in the same direction in the stock of money, and it seems highly dubious that they could. Over long periods, changes in the stock of money can in principle offset or reinforce other factors sufficiently to dominate trends in the price level.

I share, however, the doubts that the Reserve System has repeatedly expressed about the desirability of using price level stability as an immediate guide to policy. Entirely aside from the technical problem of the specific index number of prices that should be used, the key difficulty is that the link between price changes and monetary changes over short periods is too loose and too imperfectly known to make price level stability an objective and reasonably unambiguous guide to policy.

The Federal Reserve System does not control the price level. It controls the volume of its own earning assets and, at one remove under present circumstances or directly under the altered arrangements suggested in the preceding chapters, the stock of money. If the link between the stock of money and the price level were direct and rigid, or if indirect and variable, fully understood, this would be a distinction without a difference; the control of the one would imply control of the other; and it would be indifferent whether the guide to policy was stated in terms of the end to be achieved, stability of the price level, or the means to be used, changes in the stock of money. But the link is not direct and rigid, nor is it fully understood. While the stock of money is systematically related to the price level *on the average,* there is much variation in the relation over short periods of time and especially for the mild movements in both money and prices that characterize most of our experience and that we would like to have characterize all. Even the variability in the relation between money and prices would not be decisive if the link, though variable, were synchronous so that current changes in the stock of money had their full effect on economic conditions and on the price level instantaneously or with only a short lag. For it might then be fairly easy to substitute trial and error for a full understanding of the link between money and prices. Mistakes would not be cumulative and could be corrected quickly. In fact, however, there is much evidence that monetary changes have their effect only after a considerable lag and over a long period and that the lag is rather variable. In the National Bureau study on which I have been collaborating with Mrs. Schwartz, we have found that, on the average of 18 cycles, peaks in the rate of change in the stock of money tend to precede peaks in general business by about 16 months and troughs in the rate of change in the stock of money to precede troughs in general business by about 12 months. The results would be roughly comparable if the comparisons were made with peaks and troughs in a price index rather than in general business. For individual cycles, the recorded lead has varied between 6 and 29 months at peaks and between 4 and 22 months at troughs. This is highly consistent behavior as such observations go and sufficient to pin down the *average* lead within a rather narrow range. But it is highly variable behavior for the individual episode with which policy must be concerned.

Under these circumstances, the price level — or for that matter any other set of economic indicators — could be an effective guide only if it were possible to predict, first, the effects of non-monetary factors on the price level for a considerable period of time in the future, second, the length of time it will take in each particular instance for monetary actions to have their effect, and third, the amount of effect of alternative monetary actions. In the present state of our knowledge, it is hard enough to conceive of an effective trial-and-error procedure for adapting to price level movements of two, three, or four years in length if monetary action taken today uniformly had its effect over a period centered, say, 14 months from now. I find it virtually impossible to conceive of an effective procedure when there is little basis for knowing whether the lag between action and effect will be 4 months or 29 months or somewhere in between. We are probably only today experiencing the effects of the rapid expansion in the money supply in the first half of 1958 in response to the 1957–58 recession. That recession itself may well have reflected in part the relatively slow rate of increase during 1956 and 1957, in its turn a reaction to the contemporaneous rise in prices. The 1956–57 price rise was itself related to the monetary expansion in 1954 and 1955 which was a reaction to the recession of 1953–54; and so on. Though oversimplified, this portrayal has enough potential validity to illustrate the problem.

A satisfactory policy guide or rule should be connected more directly with the means available to the monetary authority than is the price level. We will, I believe, further the ultimate end of achieving a reasonably stable price level better by specifying the role of the monetary authorities in terms of magnitudes they effectively control and for whose behavior they can properly be held responsible than by instructing them solely to do the right thing at the right time when there is no clear and accepted criterion even after the event whether they have done so. In this as in so many human activities what seems the long way round may be the short way home.

The most important magnitude that the monetary authorities can effectively control and for which they have primary responsibility is the stock of money. Under present circumstances, even the stock of money is not directly controlled by the System. The System controls directly its own earning assets. . . . The total of high-powered money is affected in addition by such factors as gold flows, changes in Treasury balances, and the like; and the total money stock for any given total of high-powered money is affected by the ratio of high-powered money to deposits that banks choose to hold and the ratio of currency to deposits that the public chooses to hold. . . . The links between Reserve action and the money supply are sufficiently close, the effects occur sufficiently rapidly, and the connections are sufficiently well understood, so that reasonably close control over the money supply is feasible, given the will. I do not mean to say that the process would not involve much trial and some error but only that the errors need not be cumulative and could be corrected fairly promptly. The process involves technical problems of considerable complexity, but they are of a kind with which the System has much experience and for which the System has trained personnel.

The stock of money therefore seems to me the relevant magnitude in terms of which to formulate monetary rules and the behavior of which should be a criterion of policy performance. The question remains, what behavior of the stock of money should we seek to achieve either by instructing the monetary authorities to do so, or by designing a system under which the desired pattern would be produced automatically?

Some years ago, I suggested as one answer to this question a largely automatic framework that would link changes in the money supply to the state of the budget. Surpluses in the budget would reduce the stock of money dollar for dollar and deficits would increase the stock of money dollar for dollar. The surpluses and deficits were themselves to result from the impact of changing economic conditions on a stable tax structure and a stable expenditure policy. The tax structure and expenditure policy were to be adjusted to the activities it was desired that government should undertake and not altered in reaction to cyclical movements — this is the "stabilizing budget policy" proposed at about the same time by the Committee for Economic Development. This proposal would thus use the built-in flexibility of the federal budget as a means of producing countercyclical movements in the stock of money.

The research I have done since this proposal was published gives me no reason to doubt that it would work well; that it would provide a stable monetary background which would render major fluctuations well-nigh impossible, would not exacerbate minor fluctuations, and might even alleviate them. But I have become increasingly persuaded that the proposal is more sophisticated and complex than is necessary, that a much simpler rule would also produce highly satisfactory results and would have two great advantages: first, its simplicity would facilitate the public understanding and backing that is necessary if the rule is to provide an effective barrier to opportunistic "tinkering"; second, it would largely separate the monetary problem from the fiscal and hence would require less far-reaching reform over a narrower area.

The simpler rule is that the stock of money be increased at a fixed rate year-in and year-out without any variation in the rate of increase to meet cyclical needs. This rule could be adopted by the Reserve System itself. Alternatively, Congress could instruct the Reserve System to follow it. If it were adopted without any other changes in our monetary arrangements, the Reserve System would have much discretion in the precise techniques used to increase the stock of money and it could achieve the objective only with an appreciable though not large margin of error — perhaps one-half to one percentage point. . . .

To make the rule specific, we need (1) to define the stock of money to which it refers, (2) to state what the fixed rate of increase should be or how it should be determined, (3) to state what if any allowance should be made for intra-year or seasonal movements.

(1) I have heretofore used the term "the stock of money" as if it were self-evident. Of course it is not. There is a continuum of assets possessing in various degrees the qualities we attribute to the ideal construct of "money" and hence there is no unique way to draw a line separating "money" from "near monies"; for different purposes or at different times it may be appropriate to draw this line at different points on the continuum. In our own research we have found the most useful concept to be one that includes currency held by the public plus adjusted demand deposits plus time deposits in commercial banks but excludes time deposits in mutual savings banks, shares in savings and loan associations, and the like. The Reserve System has generally used the term "money" more narrowly, to include only currency and demand deposits, and many economists have used it more broadly, to include also time deposits in mutual savings banks. I am inclined myself to favor the concept we have used because it seems to be somewhat more closely related empirically to income and other economic magnitudes than the other concepts and because it does not require classifying the deposit liabilities of individual institutions in terms of bookkeeping categories that permit much variation. But the evidence for this concept is certainly far from conclusive. More important, I do not believe it is vital which particular concept is chosen as long as first, it is at least as broad as currency plus adjusted demand deposits; second, a definite and clear-cut choice is made; and, third, the rate of increase chosen is adapted to the concept. The possible candidates for inclusion have had different secular rates of growth and are likely to continue to do so. They do not however vary radically with respect to one another over short periods and they would vary even less if some of my earlier suggestions were adopted, in particular, payment of interest on reserve balances with the Federal Reserve, and abolition of the pres-

ent prohibition on the payment of interest on demand deposits and ceiling on the interest on time deposits.

(2) The rate of increase should be chosen so that on the average it could be expected to correspond with a roughly stable long-run level of final product prices. For the concept of money just recommended, namely, currency plus all commercial bank deposits, this would have required a rate of growth of slightly over 4% per year on the average of the past 90 years — something over 3% to allow for growth in output and 1% to allow for a secular decrease in velocity, which is to say for the increase in the stock of money per unit of output that the public has wished to hold as its real per capita income rose. To judge from this evidence, a rate of increase of 3 to 5% per year might be expected to correspond with a roughly stable price level for this particular concept of money. Since time deposits have grown in the past decade relative to demand deposits, and non-commercial bank time deposits relative to commercial, a somewhat lower rate of increase might be appropriate if a narrower definition were adopted, a somewhat higher rate, if a broader definition were adopted.

As with the definition, the particular rate of increase adopted seems to me less important than the adoption of a fixed rate provided only that the rate is somewhere in the range suggested and that it is adapted to the definition of money. A rate that turned out to be somewhat too high would mean a mild secular price rise, a rate that turned out to be somewhat too low, a mild secular price fall. Neither, it seems to me, would be serious. What is seriously disturbing to economic stability are rapid and sizable fluctuations in prices, not mild and steady secular movements in either direction. A fixed rate of increase in the stock of money would almost certainly rule out such rapid and sizable fluctuations, though it would not rule out mild cyclical or secular fluctuations, and it would give a firm basis for long range planning on the part of the public.

(3) I find the treatment of intra-year movements more puzzling. We now take for granted a seasonal movement in the stock of money and tend to assimilate it to other seasonal movements. Yet there is a crucial difference. The seasonal movement in the stock of money is a quasi-deliberate act of policy, not a product of climatic or similar circumstances. One initial objective of the Reserve System was to reduce seasonal fluctuations in interest rates. It has accomplished this objective by widening seasonal movements in the stock of money. I see no objection to seasonal variation in the stock of money, provided it is regular so that the public can adapt to it. On the other hand, neither do I see any objection to seasonal fluctuations in short-

term interest rates. While the kind of pegging involved in eliminating seasonal fluctuations in interest rates has some special justifications, it is by no means free from the defects of other kinds of pegging. Moreover, there is no way to determine at all precisely what seasonal movement is required in the stock of money to eliminate a seasonal in interest rates. The actual seasonal that has been introduced into the stock of money has been sizable and has varied considerably from year to year. Hence, the proposal, which at first sight seems attractive, to apply a regular rate of increase to the seasonally adjusted stock of money, would involve introducing an essentially arbitrary element into the behavior of the stock of money — there is no seasonal to adjust until a decision is made what seasonal to introduce. My own tentative conclusion is that it would be preferable to dispense with seasonal adjustments and to adopt the rule that the actual stock of money should grow month by month at the predetermined rate. To avoid misunderstanding, let me note explicitly that this would be consistent with seasonal movements in currency and deposits separately, as long as they offset one another.

The proposal to increase the money stock at a fixed rate month-in and month-out is certainly simple. It is likely to strike many of you as also simple-minded. Surely, you will say, it is easy to do better. Surely, it would be better to "lean against the wind," in the expressive phrase of a Federal Reserve chairman, rather than to stand straight upright whichever way the wind is blowing. Some of my previous comments perhaps suggest that the matter is not so simple. We seldom in fact know which way the economic wind is blowing until several months after the event, yet to be effective, we need to know which way the wind is going to be blowing when the measures we take now will be effective, itself a variable date that may be a half year or a year or two years from now. Leaning today against next year's wind is hardly an easy task in the present state of meteorology.

Analogies aside, the historical record gives little basis for supposing that it is an easy task to do better than the simple rule I have suggested. Since at least the early 1920's, our monetary authorities have been trying to do just that; they have been trying to use monetary policy as an instrument for promoting stability. On the whole, the persons in charge of monetary policy have been as able, public spirited, and far-sighted a group as one could reasonably hope to have in such positions, though of course there have been some exceptions in both directions, and they have been served by a research staff that has numbered some of our leading monetary scholars and has maintained a high standard of technical excellence. Yet over this period as a whole, I doubt that many, if any, informed students of monetary affairs would disagree with the judgment that the actual behavior of the money stock has clearly been decidedly worse than the behavior that would have been produced by the simple rule — and this is true even if we leave out the war-time periods when the simple rule would almost surely have been departed from and perhaps rightly so.

The simple rule would have avoided the excessive expansion of the stock of money from 1919 to 1920 and the sharp contraction thereafter, the fairly mild but steady deflationary pressure of the later 1920's, the collapse of the stock of money from 1929 to 1933, the rather rapid rise thereafter, and the sharp decline in the course of the 1937–38 recession. In the period since World War II, the simple rule would have produced a lower rate of growth in the stock of money until the end of 1946 than was in fact realized, almost the same rate of growth during 1947, a faster rate of growth from some-time in 1947 to the end of 1949, which is to say, throughout the closing phases of the 1946–48 expansion and the whole of the 1948–49 contraction. The simple rule would have produced about the same rate of growth in the stock of money as was realized on the average from 1950 to early or mid-1953; a higher rate from then to mid-1954, or throughout most of the 1953–54 recession; about the same rate as was experienced from mid-1954 to mid-1955; a somewhat higher rate from then until the end of 1957; especially in the last half of 1957, after the 1957–58 contraction got under way; a lower rate than experienced in the first half of 1958, and about the same as the rate actually experienced from then to mid-1959.

The striking improvements in the behavior of the stock of money that would have been produced by the simple rule are for the inter-war period and for the major fluctuations of that period. It is these that make me so confident that informed students would render a nearly unanimous verdict in favor of the simple rule for the period as a whole. But, rule or no rule, changes in the monetary structure — notably federal insurance of bank deposits, the altered asset structure of banks, and the altered role of gold — and changes in the attitudes of the monetary authorities — notably their heightened sensitivity to contractions — render a repetition of major mistakes like those made during the inter-war period highly unlikely. It is nearly inconceivable that the monetary authorities would now permit the money stock to decline by one-third, as it did from 1929–33, or even by nearly 4% in 10 months, as it did in 1937. It is no doubt a merit of the rule that it provides insurance against such major mistakes but it may plausibly be argued that other factors have already provided adequate insurance — though I would be tempted to add that new mistakes are legion and insurance against major mistakes differing in kind from those in the past, in particular against unduly large increases in the money supply, is well worth while.

For the period since World War II, the contrast is not nearly so clear or sharp. The monetary authorities have followed a policy that has produced a behavior of the money supply very close to its hypothetical behavior under the rule, far closer than between the wars. In consequence, a finer criterion of performance is required to judge the desirability or undesirability of such discrepancies as there are, and this is true also for the milder discrepancies in the earlier period. My own judgment is that even for these, the rule would have produced clearly superior results, but I cannot be so sure that this judgment would be widely shared as I am for the period as a whole.

To supplement my own personal judgment, I tried to devise some objective way of grading actual performance relative to hypothetical performance under the rule. The attempt failed. The reason why it failed is, I think, most instructive. It is because the attempt to give operational meaning to "better and worse performance" revealed that such formulae as "leaning against the wind" or "countercyclical changes in the money supply," with which there might be widespread agreement, have no unambiguous specific content. I suspect that this is the only reason there is such widespread agreement. Each person can read his own content into these vague statements. If one tries to translate them into specific criteria that can be used to judge actual performance *ex post*, let alone to guide performance in the future, he finds that there are a variety of alternative translations, no one of which is fully satisfactory to any one person and on no one of which would there be anything like general agreement. In answer to the question whether it would be possible to do better than the simple rule, a majority of informed students might say "yes." Further probing would, however, reveal wide variety in the specific alternative policy regarded as "better." If each of these were made as explicit as the simple rule, I doubt that there would be anything like general assent to any one.

I can best elaborate on these remarks by describing briefly my attempts. Month-by-month, I recorded whether the growth in the seasonally adjusted actual money supply was higher or lower than the growth that would have been produced by a steady 4% rate of growth. I then tried to classify the difference as in the "right" or "wrong" direction according to an objective policy criterion.

The first criterion I tried was a simple translation of "leaning against the wind," namely, that the stock of money should grow at a slower than average rate during business expansions and at a higher than average rate during business contractions. By this criterion, for eight complete peacetime reference cycles from March 1919 to April 1958 (excluding the World War II cycle from June 1938 to October 1945), actual policy was in the "right" direction in 155 months, in the "wrong" direction in 226 months; so actual policy was "better" than the rule in 41% of the months. For the period after World War II alone, the results were only slightly more favorable to actual policy according to this criterion: policy was in the "right" direction in 71 months, in the "wrong" direction in 79 months, so actual policy was better than the rule in 47% of the months.

Even if the policy criterion could be accepted, numbers like these would not be an adequate measure of performance for three very different reasons. First, and least serious given a sufficiently long span of time, they take no account of the magnitude of the difference, only the direction. Second, and more serious, they treat each month separately, taking no account of the time sequence of deviations, and therefore neglect completely cumulative effects — a given number of deviations in the "wrong" direction could have very different consequences according as they were clustered or dispersed in time. Third, and most basic, suppose the results were less extreme and that actual policy were in the "right" direction 50% of the time. Would that mean a dead heat between the two alternative policies? Not at all. The alternative to the rule involves variability in the rate of change of the money supply; if the score is 50–50, this variability is simply a disturbance that introduces instability. Hence a 50–50 score would mean that the rule would be decidedly preferable — any alternative must be "better" much more than half the time in order to offset the harm it does through introducing random variability.

The policy criterion cannot however be accepted. This is clear as soon as one goes beyond the overall results, and looks at the scoring of individual months. According to this criterion, a rate of growth higher than 4% is scored as in the wrong direction from March 1933 to May 1937. But this is absurd. Economic activity may have changed its direction of movement in March 1933 but it was still abnormally low. Surely a rule that calls for reversing policy toward "tightness" the moment a cyclical trough is reached is unsatisfactory — "ease" should be continued as long as conditions are depressed. Stating the counterpart for the peak reveals an inflationary asymmetry in reaction. There will be far less agreement that a "tight" policy should be continued beyond the peak so long as conditions are prosperous.

If, however, we follow the logic both ways, we get an alternative translation of "leaning against the wind" to the effect that the money supply should grow at a slower than average rate during periods when economic conditions are "above" normal and at a faster than average rate when economic conditions are "below" normal. For simplicity, I treated the period from mid-expansion to mid-contraction as "above" normal and from mid-contraction to mid-expansion as "below" normal. By this criterion, actual policy scored much higher, being in the right direction in 56% of 377 peacetime months for the period as a whole, and in 58% of 149 months after World War II.

Once again, examination of the month-by-month scoring raises serious doubts. In the Great Depression, for example, a less than normal rate of growth is scored as in the "right" direction from August 1929 all the way to the middle of 1931; and again more recently, from the cyclical peak in November 1948 through April 1949; and from the peak in July 1953 through January 1954. Some improvement might be made by adopting a less mechanical definition of "above" and "below" normal, such as the relation of income or industrial production, or some index of business conditions to its trend, or unemployment or prices to some "normal" level. But which should it be?

The two criteria so far described agree in classifying as "right" a less than normal rate of growth during the second half of expansion and a more than normal rate during the second half of contraction. This greatest common denominator of the two criteria is of course useless for future policy; it can, however, be used as at least a partial basis for judging past performance. By this third criterion, actual policy was in the "right" direction 45% of 183 peacetime months for the period as a whole, 55% of 75 months since the end of World War II.

But even this common denominator is not unexceptionable. Once account is taken of the lag between monetary action and its effects, it is not at all clear that it is desirable to continue a lower-than-average rate of growth right up to the cyclical peak and a higher-than-average rate of growth up to the cyclical trough. If we could, might it not be desirable to ease monetary conditions before the peak and start tightening before the trough? Once again, reactions are likely to display an inflationary asymmetry — we readily agree at the peak, but many are likely to question the desirability of tightening before the trough is reached.

Still another range of possibilities is opened up by allowing not only for leads but also for a modified "needs of trade" argument. It has been argued that meeting a contraction arising from non-monetary forces with a larger than normal rate of increase in the money supply floods the market with liquidity, encourages investment in housing and other areas that is not viable in the longer run, and stimulates "speculation." In these ways, it creates difficulties for the future. Reverse phenomena are said to occur in the expansion. On this view, the appropriate behavior of the money supply is to move with the wind but only mildly; to grow at a slower rate than normal during at least the early stages of contraction and at a faster rate than normal during at least part of the expansion.

The diversity and ambiguity concealed by the phrase "counter-cyclical monetary policy" itself raises something of a puzzle. How is it that there can yet be wide consensus in retrospective judgments of the major fluctuations? The answer, I conjecture, is that these involved *large* movements and that whatever the precise pattern specified, there would be general agreement that the rate of growth of the stock of money should not deviate far from some long-run average rate of growth. If this be so, then the simple rule I have proposed itself embodies an element that is common to most views about the appropriate behavior of the stock of money, is itself something of a greatest common denominator.

But whether this be the explanation or not, one thing seems clear. There is not currently any well-defined alternative to the rule I have suggested that would command wide assent, unless it be "let the Federal Reserve System do it"; and even for this alternative, there is no well-defined criterion with which there would be wide agreement for judging *ex post* whether "they" have done "it" well or poorly.

In summing up this discussion of the appropriate behavior of the money stock, I am tempted to paraphrase what Colin Clark once wrote about the case for free trade. Like other academicians, I am accustomed to being met with the refrain, "It's all right in theory but it won't work in practice." Aside from the questionable logic of the remark in general, in this instance almost the reverse of what is intended is true. There is little to be said in theory for the rule that the money supply should grow at a constant rate. The case for it is entirely that it would work in practice. There are persuasive theoretical grounds for desiring to vary the rate of growth to offset other factors. The difficulty is that, in practice, we do not know when to do so and by how much. In practice, therefore, deviations from the simple rule have been destabilizing rather than the reverse.

I should like to emphasize that I do not regard steady growth in the money stock as the be-all and end-all of monetary policy for

all time. It is a rule that has much to recommend it in the present
state of our knowledge. It would avoid the major mistakes that have
marred our past record. It would assure long-run stability in the
purchasing power of the dollar. But I should hope that as we operated under it we would accumulate more evidence and learn to
understand more fully the workings of the monetary mechanism.
As we did so, we could perhaps devise still better rules for controlling
the stock of money that could command widespread professional
support and public understanding.

ABBA P. LERNER

Milton Friedman's A *Program for*
Monetary Stability: A Review*

Professor Lerner takes sharp issue with Friedman's recommendation
for rules instead of discretion in monetary policy. Reviewing the
twenty-three cases over the last century in which Friedman argues
that discretionary monetary policy was destabilizing, Lerner contends
that only three are instances where a mistake was made which might
be repeated, and even these he finds doubtful. He also objects to
Friedman's program to iron out business cycles, allowing the economy
to operate close to a trend line, which may involve considerable
unemployment. Lerner prefers instead the more ambitious goal of
aiming for full employment (allowing, perhaps, for 2 percent unemployed). Lerner also takes issue with Friedman's preoccupation with
a limited role for government and argues that Friedman arrives at
his conclusions essentially because of his antagonism to any discretionary government action. Lerner suggests that Friedman might well

* From *Journal of the American Statistical Association*, Vol. 57 (March
1962), pp. 211–20. Reprinted by permission of the American Statistical
Association.

be opposed to discretionary government action even if he agreed it was beneficial for the economy. In fairness to Friedman, though, it should be pointed out that in this particular instance of supporting rules over discretion in monetary policy, he believes that discretionary action yields poorer economic results than would his rule. Finally, Lerner points out that Friedman's monetary rule does not make necessary allowance for short-run changes in velocity. According to Lerner, such changes can lead to substantial cumulative fluctuations in the economy, fluctuations which would be offset not by a constant increase in the money supply but only by a change in the appropriate direction sufficient to offset that of velocity. In short, Lerner argues that the monetary authorities have to concern themselves with changes in the total volume of spending and this cannot be equated with changes in the money supply alone. It will be recalled that this point concerning the instability of velocity was also raised by Warren L. Smith in a prior selection.

Mᴏʀᴇ than twenty years ago I wrote a parable[1] in which an economy that lacked an adequate mechanism for regulating the level of effective demand was represented by an automobile built without a steering wheel. It ran on a highway with raised edges, so that if a car tended to go off the road the raised edges turned the front wheels, sending it back again in a dangerous zigzag. In that parable the suggestion of a steering wheel for the automobile was opposed by a passenger, "Suppose we had a steering wheel," he protested, "and somebody held on to it when we reached a curb! He would prevent the automatic turning of the wheel, and we would surely be overturned. And besides, we believe in democracy and cannot give anyone the extreme authority of life and death over all the occupants of the car. That would be dictatorship."[2]

I had often thought that the parable was overplayed, but Professor Milton Friedman's recent book is essentially a very sophisticated

[1] "The Economic Steering Wheel," *The University Review* (Kansas City, Missouri), June 1941, reprinted as Chapter 1 of *The Economics of Employment*, McGraw-Hill, 1951.

[2] *The Economics of Employment*, pp. 3–4.

presentation of the position of the objector to the steering wheel. "What we need," he says, "is not a skilled monetary driver of the economic vehicle continuously turning the steering wheel to adjust to unexpected irregularities of the route, but some means of keeping the monetary passenger, who is in the back seat as ballast, from occasionally leaning over and giving the steering wheel a jerk that threatens to send the car off the road."

Friedman begins by insisting that "money is important." Somewhat surprisingly, the declaration is directed not against the classical economists who, in the quantity theory of money, stressed the unimportance of money as "merely a veil" which tended to obscure the important relative price relationships and affected only the general price level, but against the "Keynesians" whose main concern — following Keynes' "The General Theory of Employment, Interest, and Money" — is with the importance of the money supply for interest, investment and employment. But this becomes understandable when it is realized (a) that Friedman deals in a version of the quantity theory of money, which takes account of the effects of the quantity of money on income and on employment as well as on the price level (so that anyone who thinks money is important is a quantity theorist), and (b) that his "Keynesianism" is a contracted version which covers only the special case of deep depression.

In a deep depression the bulk of the Keynesian analysis does not apply. The advantages of hard cash create a bottomless "liquidity trap" that prevents monetary expansion from reducing an already very low rate of interest, while a breakdown of confidence prevents any feasible reduction in the rate of interest from inducing any substantial increase in investment. The quantity of money does not have the normal "Keynesian" effects on employment via interest and investment. Money is unimportant in the sense that *monetary policy* does not work. Depression can be alleviated only by increases in direct government spending or by decreases in government taxation — namely, only by *fiscal policy*, resort to which is then prescribed by Keynes. Friedman's declaration that "Money is Important" amounts to an emphatic, if unnecessary, denial of the general validity of this special case.

The next step is to point out that during the last century the supply of money has been managed very badly. Inflations and depressions have been aggravated by changes in the quantity of money in the wrong direction. Friedman measures the instability of (the growth of) the money stock by its departure from a constant geometric rate of increase. He finds that this instability was greater after

the establishment of the Federal Reserve System than before;[3] and
the same is true of economic conditions even if the war years are
omitted — "The thirty-three peace time years after World War I were
among the most economically unstable in our history." Worse still,
a detailed analysis of the departures of the actual changes in money
stocks from a constant rate of increase, departures which are presumed
to reflect attempts to guide the economy counter-cyclically, show these
to be departures in the wrong direction more than half the time.

Friedman's conclusion is that since attempts to regulate the level
of effective demand have worked so badly it would be best to give up
the attempt. We should depend on the price mechanism to bring
about what adjustments it can, reconcile ourselves to "normal" business cycles which we have had with us always, and will continue to
have, and concentrate on preventing the aggravation of the cycles by
perverse changes in the quantity of money.

This could be achieved most simply by preventing *all* changes
in the quantity of money — simply freezing the money stock. But
there is a secular increase in the need for money on account of the
continuing increase in population, in per-capita output and income,
and in the proportion of the increased income directed to liquidity.
This continually increasing demand for money would then call for a
continually falling price level. Friedman proposes to satisfy the secular increase in the demand for money by a parallel secular increase
in the supply of money of 4 per cent per annum, or about one-third
of one per cent every month, which would be compatible with a stable
price level. But more than this we should not attempt. We know so
little about the *degree* to which any of our actions affect the level of
economic activity, or about the *time lags* involved, that we are likely to
aggravate the remaining cyclical fluctuations in economic activity if
we try to eliminate or even to mitigate them. This, he charges, is just
what has happened during the last century.

The impact of this simple argument is much strengthened by
Friedman's excellent treatment of a number of related problems.
Basing himself on the liberal principle of neutrality by the govern-
ment where its intervention would reduce the freedom of individual

[3] A minor point: In measuring the degree of monetary instability before the
establishment of the Federal Reserve System, Friedman has to interpolate to get
a number for the amount of money for some of the years in the earlier period.
This amounts to assuming that the growth of the money stock was perfectly
smooth during the years between those for which the data exists, and one won-
ders how much this contributes to making the earlier years appear more stable
than those after the Federal Reserve System was established.

consumers or investors, he provides a strikingly clear statement why the supply of money, like the enforcement of contracts and other rules without which the free market mechanism cannot work, cannot be left to the free market but must remain a responsibility of the government. He then very neatly disposes of a number of fallacies that have confused monetary issues over the years — from the "real bills doctrine" of a century ago to the more recent notion that borrowing by the government from the commercial banks increases their ability to create money (whereas it merely replaces cash with government securities that are no more than as good as cash)[4] — and boldly shows how we would benefit by freeing ourselves from what we have left of the gold standard. He has an excellent discussion of the necessary relationships between the Central Bank and the Government (or the Treasury), showing how a Central Bank can be most useful if it is neither completely subservient to the Government — as the Federal Reserve was recently when it had to peg the rate of return on government bonds — nor so completely independent as to be able to nullify the activities and the policies of the Treasury. Particularly neat in this area is his treatment of the proper relationship of the Treasury to the Federal Reserve in the management of the National Debt, where he makes a good case for the Government's limiting itself to quite short- and quite long-term borrowing and the undesirability of its trying to tailor the kind of loan to the state of the markets.

Extremely impressive, too, is his explanation of how the effectiveness of the Federal Reserve System could be increased by *reducing* the number of its instruments — in particular, by limiting it to open market operations and taking away its control over reserve requirements, which is too strong an instrument to be practical, somewhat reminiscent of countries that find themselves internationally impotent because their H bombs are too powerful to be used.

In this connection he properly criticizes the error of treating *unrequired* reserves (i.e., excess reserves) as *undesired* reserves whose disappearance would not be felt and providing no offset to the reduction in the excess of actual over required reserves when reserve requirements were increased.

Friedman comes out in favor of a 100 per cent reserve system (which would incidentally make Federal Deposit Insurance unnecessary) and proposes to meet some of the financial objections raised

---

[4] He seems to go too far in implying that government borrowing from the public could never be expected to induce more thrift than borrowing from the commercial banks, but his tendency to disregard effects that involve changes in the velocity of circulation is discussed below.

in the past against this proposal by having the government not only provide the additional money needed to bring actual reserves up to 100 per cent, but also pay interest to banks on their reserves at the current rate of interest, the banks being permitted to pay interest on deposits. Friedman justifies this in part by arguing that consumers who release productive resources in order to hold money should be rewarded just as much as those who release productive resources to hold securities, but he also takes account of the less questionable consideration that the earnings of interest on deposits would make liquidity cheaper so the public could enjoy more of it. This would set free those resources, like bookkeeping services, whose function it is to economize on liquidity, and this would result in a net social gain, since no social cost is involved in providing a larger stock of (paper or bookkeeping) money. If competition between the banks raised the rate of interest paid on deposits to equality with the current rate of interest on gilt-edged securities (perhaps partly paid in the form of banking services), the cost of liquidity would be reduced to zero and the quantity of money held would be that which reduced the marginal utility of liquidity to zero and maximized the total enjoyment of liquidity by society.

Throughout all of these side issues one can see flowing the pure milk of economic liberalism applied with the distinguished expository and analytical skill which we have come to expect from the author. This is combined with a daring disregard of popular superstitions, often even when very strong, such as in his perfectly logical demonstration that it is not more objectionable to keep (the rate of increase in) the amount of money constant through the seasons of the year and to experience seasonal variations in the rate of interest instead of the traditional seasonal variation in the quantity of money. On all of these I find myself in very close sympathy with Friedman. Indeed, I would even go a little further in one or two cases, where he somewhat suddenly seeks to make concessions to public opinion.

Having pointed out that the most sensible thing for a government is to borrow either very short or through perpetuities, he suggests as a compromise with the antipathy to consols or perpetuities that the government should issue eight- or nine-year bonds instead. If these could remain eight- or nine-year bonds all the time, the concession would not be serious. But time passes. There would exist bonds of every length of maturity on the open market where the managers of the national debt would have to operate. The neat and attractive simplicity of the simple choice between long and short is lost by the concession.

He could make the argument for the advantages of 100 per cent reserves over Federal Deposit Insurance more impressive by pointing out that it has similarities to *self insurance,* with the special advantage that it yields the economies of eliminating the need for the additional accounting and supervision involved in Federal Deposit Insurance while it avoids the normal costs and risks of self insurance because of the peculiar quality of paper, bookkeeping or credit moneys (as distinct from commodity moneys like gold) that their provision involves no social cost.

Friedman limits his proposal for the payment of interest on money to *deposit* money, where the interest would be credited to the accounts by the bank, but there is no good reason for leaving out cash from this benefit. It would be perfectly easy for the government to pay interest on the cash too by simply giving every holder of a dollar bill a three- or four-cent present every Christmas (or a one cent bonus three or four times a year) while stamping a date or punching a hole in the dollar as a check. This would make *all* liquidity free and avoid the wasteful substitution of interest-earning bank deposits for non-interest-earning cash where cash is more convenient.

Of greater interest is Friedman's failure to see that his proposal to have interest paid on bank reserves and on bank deposits would make it unnecessary for him to choose seasonal fluctuations in the rate of interest instead of the more conventional seasonal changes in the quantity of money. With liquidity made free it would cost nothing to hold throughout the year the extra money needed only in certain seasons. There would then be no more need to change either the rate of interest or the amount of money for fluctuations in seasonal needs for money than for the much greater fluctuations in the need for money in the daytime as compared with the night.

The same development would also affect the long-term — short-term problems in the management of the national debt. The short-term rate of interest is generally lower than the long-term rate of interest because a short-term security has greater liquidity, and it is the demand for this liquidity that raises the market price of the short-term security as compared with the price of the long-term security, and thus makes it show a lower rate of yield. If liquidity were made free, as it would be by Friedman's proposal to make the interest paid on money held equal to the current rate of interest on gilt-edged securities, the general excess of the long-term rate over the short-term rate would disappear, and there would remain only the difference due to the long-term rate being an average of the short-term rates over the long-term period and therefore not fluctuating as much as the short-term rate.

But even a more than one hundred per cent agreement with Friedman's incidental contributions to the analysis of monetary theory and the mechanics of monetary policy fails to prevent a mounting skepticism about his main thesis that for fear of making things worse rather than better we should limit our policy to stabilizing the rate of increase of the money stock. For this there are three reasons.

In the first place, Friedman is much too successful in pointing out the nature of the errors in monetary management and fiscal policy during the last century, which he considers to have aggravated rather than ameliorated the "natural" cyclical fluctuations. While his theoretical argument runs in terms of the impossibility of forecasting accurately, almost all the actual errors made turn out to be errors which would certainly not have been made by Friedman if he were in charge of the Treasury or the Federal Reserve.

Friedman's summary analysis of the policy errors that worked the wrong way during the last century contains 23 instances. Four of these are cases of inflation during war time, which fall outside the present discussion. There are seven cases of decreases in the quantity of money from bank collapses. These have no relevance to a future where such happenings are rendered almost harmless by Federal Deposit Insurance and would be completely prevented by Friedman's one hundred per cent reserve program. There are five cases where obviously wrong policies were forced upon the government by the exigencies of the Gold Standard. Following Friedman's proposal for freeing the country from the incubus of the remnants of the Gold Standard, these, too, fall out of the picture. There are four cases where a definitely wrong policy was freely chosen, but the policies are recognizable as wrong without benefit of hindsight and their perpetrators are quite properly chided by Friedman — for pegging short-term or long-term rates of interest or doubling reserve requirements of commercial banks and expecting this to have no effect on the liquidity of the economy.

There remain, in all, three cases out of the twenty-three where the mistake is one that might be repeated, and even that does not seem too likely. These three cases consist of the inadequate and belated action of the Federal Reserve System in buying only one billion dollars worth of government bonds in 1932, the inactivity of the Federal Reserve in 1933 and the fall in the quantity of money and in prices in the recession of 1948–49.

From this recession to the present time there has been fair stability. This may be due, as Friedman suggests, to a vague recognition by the authorities of the desirability of maintaining a constant

rate of growth in the money supply, or it may be that Federal Deposit
Insurance and the weakening of Gold Standard pressures have removed the causes of monetary instability uncovered by Friedman in
the history of the last century.

In the second place, Friedman's measure of the appropriateness
or perversity of the departures from a constant rate of increase in the
money stock are vitiated by his basing his criterion on the phase in the
business cycle. He is very critical of proponents of monetary and fiscal
policies for full employment who "ignore" the business cycle. I
would be in favor of ignoring the business cycle if this means rejecting
the "ironing out" of the business cycle as the objective of policy in
favor of maintaining full employment without inflation, taking the
view that the business cycle is something which we do not need and
can manage very well without — that it is what happens to the economy if there is no policy for maintaining full employment.

Friedman's preoccupation with the business cycle leads him to
adopt as his test of the appropriate direction of departures from a
constant increase in the quantity of money not whether the measures
taken were calculated to bring the economy closer to full employment
without inflation, but whether they were countercyclical or not.
Friedman checks this with the stage of the business cycle — i.e.,
whether one is in a rising or declining phase of the cycle or whether
one is in an upper or lower half. A perfect score by these criteria
would be obtained not by a policy that produced full employment
without inflation, but by one that had no effect whatever on the
over-all level of economic activity yet eliminated the cycles or waves
in economic activity, either by making the actual level of employment
coincide exactly with the trend line, or by evening out the level of
activity in each cycle to a horizontal line, producing a step curve of
economic development. Which of these was achieved would depend
on whether it was the deviation from the trend that was the criterion
or whether it was the deviation from the average level of activity
in the cycle.

To one not so obsessed by the business cycle it would seem more
reasonable to compare the actual situation with full employment,
calling for more spending (possibly via more money) whenever there
was less than full employment, and for less spending (possibly via
less money) whenever there was inflation from excess demand; and
for the regulation of administered prices when there was inflation due
to the increase of administered prices in the absence of excess demand.
For this purpose full employment might initially be defined as two
per cent unemployment, the definition to be refined with experience

by bringing in such things as data on vacancies, wage differentials, hours worked per week, profit margins, etc.

In the third place Friedman's main argument can appear convincing or even plausible only to those who share his extreme — I would even say anarchistic — opposition to discretionary governmental authority. At first this shows itself in an extreme emphasis on the quantity of money, not only as the determinant of the level of economic activity, but as a measure of the degree of success of monetary policy — almost as if stability of the rate of growth of the quantity of money was identical with the stability of the economy. Right in the beginning of the book there is a formula that describes how the quantity of money is regulated by the Federal Reserve through its operation on "hard money," that is, of cash and of bank reserves and on the ratio of total money to hard money. There is nothing illegitimate in this procedure but it does have the effect of pushing further into the background the possibility of fluctuation in the volume of expenditure, which, seen as a ratio to the amount of money, is now two ratios removed from the "hard money" controlled by monetary policy. One's discomfort at the concentration on the quantity of money is increased by Friedman's insistence that the *right definition* of an "easy money" policy must run in terms of its effect on the quantity of money, and his attack on the use of the term for a policy of keeping the rate of interest low where this does not result in increasing the quantity of money, declaring that "a tendency to regard the absolute level of the discount rate . . . as a measure of 'tightness' or 'ease' has been perhaps the single most pervasive source of confusion and error in the [Federal Reserve] System's experience." It is difficult to avoid the impression that Friedman's insistence on *the right definition* is a reflection of his conviction that it is only a departure from *the right policy* that makes money really too easy (or too tight). This is perilously close to smuggling one's conclusions into one's definitions and even reminiscent of the perhaps apocryphal story of the crude quantity theorist in the thirties, who, repeatedly disappointed in his prognoses of inflation as the money stock increased, saved the day by *defining* inflation as an increase in the quantity of money.

But Friedman is no *crude* quantity theorist. His concentration on the quantity of money is due to no confusion of definitions with prognoses or with policy, but to an eagerness for a policy which is independent of discretionary action by government. The force behind Friedman's continuing to fear the evils of the dead bogies of the past, against which he, himself, has proposed most effective protection, is his extraordinary antipathy to government responsibility or fear of governmental discretionary authority. This is the influence, operating on the inevitable weighting of imponderables that is involved in passing from analysis to policy, that causes an analyst as careful as Friedman to favor a formulation that, by making it easier to forget the problem of fluctuations in the velocity of circulation, makes it easier to hold that discretion may be dispensed with, and even to forget some of his own contributions to economic understanding.

Thus in properly criticizing the Federal Reserve's doubling reserve requirements in 1936–37, without doing anything to offset the resulting extinction of excess reserves, he points out that for neutrality substitute reserves must be provided of somewhere between zero and 100 per cent of the extinguished reserves, depending on the degree to which they have been desired. Yet in his proposal for 100 per cent reserves, he assumes that it would be appropriate to supply just 100 per cent of the increase in reserves required to cover the existing volume of deposits at the 100 per cent rate. Much more than this would be necessary because of his accompanying suggestion that interest be paid on deposits. This, by making liquidity much cheaper if not free, would greatly increase the demand for money. Nowhere does Friedman treat of the need for being prepared to supply the additional amounts of money which would be demanded under such circumstances, even though there is here much more than the *possibility* of an important decline in the velocity of circulation.

Friedman's anarchism would seem to be based not on the premise that men are naturally good and wise but on the axiom that governments are naturally foolish and evil, so that even what looks like a purely beneficial governmental economic activity should be regarded as a dangerous evil, to avoid which it is worthwhile making serious sacrifices. This makes it possible for him to find "merit" in the suggestion that banking be completely free from government regulation, even after his own brilliant account of the "inherent instability" of an unregulated banking system. He treats the interference with individual freedom from the government intervention involved in Federal Deposit Insurance as of the same order of significance as the "widespread liquidity crises involving runs on banks, banking panics, suspension of convertibility of deposits into currency and rest and . . . drastic liquidation and ultimate collapse of the banking system" that, in his own words, are threatened by unregulated banking. In his eagerness to grasp the possibility of avoiding the even smaller degree of government intervention involved in 100 per cent reserve requirements, he commends a judicial balancing of this evil against the avoidance of "widespread liquidity crises, etc.," with the hope that perhaps in modern times these would not be quite as frequent or as severe as they were in the past.

There is one sense in which Friedman's approach is very strictly Keynesian. Unlike the classical economists he does not want to depend on price flexibility to bring about the needed increases in the real money stock via reductions in the price level, but wishes to have the nominal quantity of money increased instead. Like Keynes, he recognizes the existence of price rigidities which would make the price reduction route unpractical. Again, like Keynes, he sees the failure of the fully automatic price mechanism only in a rigidity of prices *downward* and pays no attention to the possibility of a closely related defect which tends to make prices rise. In short, there is no consideration of cost-push or seller's inflation or administered inflation — i.e., of the condition in which prices rise even though there is no excess demand. If there were no such thing as administered inflation, a proper regulation of the level of spending would suffice to have the economy running at a satisfactory level without inflation. The only question would then be whether the appropriate level of spending is best achieved by a discretionary monetary and fiscal policy or by following a non-discretionary rule like Friedman's. But the recognition of the existence of inflationary pressures besides that from excess demand has important implications for the central question — What would happen if the United States were to adopt Friedman's Rule?

In the first place, it is clear that we would not have such aggravations of business cycles as would be caused by perverse changes in the rate of increase of the quantity of money, but it seems almost as certain that we have now reached a stage of development in which we would avoid such perverse movements in the quantity of money in any case.

In the second place, the long run tendency — under Friedman's Rule as well as under a discretionary policy limited to checking inflation and deflation by monetary fiscal measures — would be not towards full employment but towards that level of unemployment which results in stability of the general price level. In the United States the price-stability level of unemployment seems to be something like seven per cent. With a discretionary monetary and fiscal policy, if anything happens to reduce unemployment below this level, prices would rise and steps would be taken to reduce effective demand (so as to stop the inflation) until the demand was no greater than that which gave the price-stability level of unemployment.

If there should be less demand than this, there would be no inflation (and even possibly some tendency for prices to fall). Steps would then be taken to increase effective demand (so as to reduce the level of unemployment) until the price-stability level of unemployment had been passed, when the expansion of effective demand would be stopped by the induced rise in prices and the fear of inflation.

Under the Friedman Rule a level of employment above the price-stability level (which is the same thing as a level of *unemployment* below the price-stability level) would result in rising prices. Since the nominal money stock would not react to this, the result would be a decrease in (the rate of increase of) the real money stock that ultimately would bring demand and employment down to the price-stability level. Similarly, if demand fell below the price-stability level, the undisturbed constant secular rate of growth in the quantity of money would tend ultimately to raise demand to the price-stability level.[5] It could never do more than that because if it did prices would rise and the Rule would work to *reduce* demand.

In the third place, it still seems most unplausible that discretionary monetary and fiscal policies could not do considerably better than Friedman's Rule if there should be any fluctuations in the need for money that could be offset and prevented from becoming cumulative by reasonable adjustments either in the money supply or in government taxing or spending.

In the case of demand greater than the price-stability level, Friedman's Rule would probably not work as quickly or as certainly as discretionary fiscal-monetary policy because the corrective movement — the increase in the price level — could be quite slow and could establish a self-sustaining expectation of continuing price increases fed out of increased demand out of dishoarding (increases in the velocity of circulation) which the Rule on principle does nothing about. While this must ultimately come to an end when the money stock becomes inadequate, inflation could proceed a very long way before it was checked and it would then result in a correspondingly violent deflationary reaction.

If demand should fall below the price stability level, whether as a reaction to a boom or for any other reason, the Rule would again, on principle, do nothing. Since in our asymmetrical world this would not lead to falling prices (short of a very severe depression and perhaps not even then) there would not be even the slow-motion automatic correction such as there is for a demand above the price-stability

---

[5] Unless the rate of growth in the need for money at the depressed level of the economy was as great as the rate of growth in each supply — e.g., if the depressed economy stayed at 90 per cent of potential, actual and potential increasing together at, say, 4 per cent per annum.

level. Given enough time the continued secular increase in the money supply would probably result in an ultimate increase in demand because an economy depressed below the price-stability level would probably have a lower rate of growth, but there would be even greater possibilities of depression feeding on itself (decreasing velocity of circulation) and the most probable result would be the abandonment of the Rule under pressure for some positive anti-depression action.

I would therefore expect the *average* level of employment to be lower under the Friedman Rule than with a discretionary, price-level stabilizing, monetary fiscal policy. But even the latter would have us lose something like 50 billion dollars per annum of potential output, and more than that as the potentiality of the economy grew, as long as inflationary pressures on the supply side — administered inflation not due to excess demand — is countered only by (discretionary or slow-motion automatic) decreases in demand.

In the fourth place there are additional reasons for expecting greater instability in the level of economic activity. Even though the total money *stock* would be prevented from misbehaving by Friedman's Rule, there is nothing in it to prevent important variations in the velocity of circulation. What is very strange here is that while Friedman has little use for the notion of a liquidity trap which would make it possible for a decline in demand due to a moderate recession from becoming progressive, his suggestion for paying interest on deposits would have the effect of bringing into being a much greater and more frightening source of instability than any which exists at the present time or which existed during the depression of the 1930's.

Many amateur economists have expressed concern for the dangers arising out of the possibility of consumers and investors holding on to cash instead of spending it. They have therefore proposed taxing bank deposits and making holders of currency purchase stamps in order to retain the validity of their money. These fears have usually been disregarded by professional economists who point out that there already exists an inducement for people to spend their money rather than to hold on to it, namely, the interest which is foregone in holding money (though Keynes' liquidity trap concedes that in some conditions this inducement is inadequate).

While money-taxers, like Gesell and Dahlberg, tend to be scorned by the profession, a closely related point has been made by Professor William Vickrey in discussing the advantages and disadvantages of cheap liquidity. With liquidity made costless, or at least very cheap, by the earning of interest on money held, the public will "buy" much more liquidity by holding larger money stocks. With a larger quantity of money being held, a great deal of it will not be needed very urgently so that people could easily be induced to vary the amount they want to hold.[6] This could result in considerable changes in the desired rate of spending — changes that would have to be prevented or offset for economic stability. Vickrey points out that though there is no significant social cost involved in providing the extra money, whether in the form of bank deposits or paper currency, that yields the extra enjoyment of liquidity, there may be a very serious social cost if the fluctuations in desire or need for liquidity make it much more difficult to stabilize the level of effective demand and of economic activity.

This leads Vickrey, perhaps somewhat playfully, to defend inflation as "stabilizing." Inflation *reduces* the enjoyment of liquidity by discouraging the holding of (depreciating) money beyond what is really necessary, and thereby increases the stability of the demand for money and of the whole economy.[7]

Coming back to Friedman we see that though his central Rule outlaws all attempts to offset changes in velocity of circulation, his proposed liberation of liquidity (by paying interest on money) would make the velocity of circulation much more unstable than ever. I find myself in favor of Friedman's proposal for making liquidity a free good, but I would be strongly against it if I believed, as Friedman does, that we cannot and should not try to do anything to manage or offset the resulting instabilities in the propensity to spend. He has done well in suggesting improved techniques and instruments for

[6] This is not the same as a "liquidity trap" (which is a high response in demand for liquidity with respect to changes in the rate of interest), but a high response in the demand for liquidity with respect to many *other* changes in the over-all situation — not necessarily a high elasticity of the liquidity curve (which would show itself in large shifts from money to other investments in response to small changes in alternative earnings not immediately balanced by changes in the interest earned on money held) but a high volatility of the curve itself to small changes in, say, the attractiveness of newly available durable consumption goods or rumors as to the availability of special bargains or investment opportunities. I am indebted for clarification on this point to discussions at the Money Workshop at Michigan State University and especially to further conversation with my colleague Professor Boris Pesek.

[7] Vickrey is, of course, assuming that proper institutional arrangements have been made so that little harm is done by the rising prices, all contracts, wages, pensions, rents, etc., being adjusted to the rising prices. It would seem to be much easier to obtain Vickrey's benefits by a policy of stable prices together with a tax on money *a la* Gesell.

regulating the volume of money, and in clarifying the understanding of how the improved techniques and instruments could be used. He makes a strong case for having the Federal Reserve concentrate on regulating the money supply, but he does not make a plausible case for throwing away the increased understanding and power, and more, by submitting to his Rule.

JOHN KAREKEN AND ROBERT M. SOLOW

Lags in Monetary Policy*

In the preceding selection, Lerner criticizes what he calls Friedman's obsession with rules rather than discretion. He does not, however, discuss Friedman's important point about lags in the economic effects of monetary changes. A critical evaluation of the validity of Friedman's conclusion is made in the selection below. The authors first question the logic of Friedman's approach. The fact that monetary changes precede changes in general economic conditions by twelve or sixteen months or any other period is no proof of causal relationship. One has to make some assumption as to what would have happened if other monetary policies had been followed. In addition, the authors criticize Friedman's choice of variables, arguing that it is just as appropriate to use the stock of money rather than its rate of change as an indicator of economic policy. Even better, they suggest, is to relate the specific policy measures of the monetary authorities to changes in other economic variables. In fact, when the authors relate changes in the supply of money with changes in aggregate output, they find no discernible lag. For the most part, the two variables move simultaneously; to the extent that there is any evidence of a lag in change of economic activity behind monetary changes, its duration is

* From the Commission on Money and Credit, *Stabilization Policies*, pp. 2–24. © 1963. Reprinted by permission of Prentice-Hall, Inc., Englewood Cliffs, New Jersey.

about three months. The authors do not claim that their analysis provides a strong case for discretionary monetary policy; they suggest, rather, the more negative conclusion that such policy cannot be ruled out as ineffective due to the alleged long lags between monetary change and economic effects. Their own conclusion is that the degree of effectiveness of discretionary monetary policy is still very much an open question.

WE begin with one negative result. The only widely-believed, systematic assertion currently on the books about monetary-policy lags is Milton Friedman's proposition that the effects of monetary policy actions on aggregate output are powerful, but occur with a very long and highly variable lag — of the order of a year and a half. If this were true, it would be an extremely damaging attack on discretionary monetary policy. We have come to the conclusion, though, that this proposition simply will not hold water. We believe that the method underlying the proposition is based on a *non sequitur,* and further we have convincing evidence that all or most of the Friedman lag is a statistical artifact, arising because he compares the *rate of change* of the money supply with the *level* of economic activity. When correction is made for the bias inherent in this comparison, no systematic lag appears. But since we believe that whole Friedman approach to be faulty, we do not conclude from this that monetary policy works instantaneously.

In searching for positive conclusions, we have found it convenient to think in terms of three lags or stages in the operation of monetary policy. First, there is an "inside" lag, a lapse of time between the moment when there is need for a change in policy (as recognized afterwards) and the moment when the Federal Reserve acts. One could subdivide this lag into a "recognition" lag and an "action" or "decision" lag, but it seems clear that the recognition lag is the important one. Second, there is a lag between the moment when an action is taken by the Federal Reserve and the moment when the banking system begins to be faced with changed conditions. To illustrate: reserves created by open-market purchases may initially be extinguished by a reduction in member bank indebtedness to the System. Ultimately, the Federal Reserve has its way with total reserves, but there is a lag or slippage. (Of course, free reserves respond right away; yet free reserves may not be everything.) As a second example, the Federal Reserve's operations on bank liquidity take some time to be reflected in interest rates. (Whether other credit terms respond more quickly and more significantly is *unknown*. Much is said offhand, but no quantitative knowledge appears to exist; this is a crucial subject for further research.) Third, there is an outside lag; even after firms and households are confronted with a changed supply of money and credit, there is an inevitable lag before real output can be significantly affected.

In speaking of these various lags, we do not mean to suggest a discrete gap, like the lag between lightning and thunder. Only in the case of the inside lag is a discrete lag very meaningful. In the other cases we presume that there is an *ultimate* long-run effect, which is built up gradually. We are trying to measure this distributed lag.

The inside lag of (classical) monetary policy, as noted previously, is the lapse of time between the need, somehow defined, for a major reversal of the emphasis of policy and the taking of action. As was also noted above, we have some evidence to suggest that the lapse of time between the recognition of the need for change and the taking of action is pretty nearly zero, so that the inside lag is in effect a recognition lag.

The need for a change in policy can be dated by taking the months in which turning points — either National Bureau turning points, or those in individual time series — occur. Peaks signal the need for a switch to easy money, and troughs the need for a switch to tight money. Thus, using abrupt changes in a variable $E(t)$, member bank lending capacity, to date the taking of action, we get two types of inside lags: type 1, the lag from peak to the switch to easy money, and type 2, the lag from trough to the switch to tight money.

For the post-Accord period, the average type 1 lag is about eight months; the average type 2 lag is about three months. We believe this discrepancy can be accounted for by the Federal Reserve's concern for the behavior of prices, and so are inclined to take the three month estimate as a reasonable upper bound on the inside lag.

Of course, the need for a change of policy can be defined in many ways. Trying alternative definitions, we found no reason to modify the above conclusion. Nor did our investigation of the pre-Accord period suggest the need for modification.

On the question of the intermediate lag between Federal Reserve action and response within the banking system, we have investigated two somewhat different aspects. The first is straightforward. Leaving aside all outside factors, we can simply imagine the Federal Reserve as trying to control the gross reserves (inclusive of borrowed reserves) of the member banks by operating on their net reserves (exclusive of borrowing). It appears from our analysis that the Federal Reserve can have its way with gross reserves essentially within a month or so. Whether this is accomplished by clever open-market policy or by stern looks at the discount window is from our point of view immaterial. The relation is close and quick.

We come now to a very different aspect of the intermediate lag. We have tried to explain (and observe the time of) *changes* in the average interest rate on short-term bank loans to business as a response to the balance of demand for and supply of credit, the former coming essentially from outside the banking system and the latter governed essentially by the monetary authorities. We have not had much success, and we think this question needs to be pursued further. The best relation we have found is perfectly reasonable in outline, but it explains less than half of the variance of changes in interest rates. No doubt this could be improved, and we make suggestions for later experimentation. If our not very encouraging regression equation can be taken at all seriously, it suggests (a) that the Federal Reserve can offset disturbances to the credit market emanating from elsewhere, but (b) that the process of equilibration of the credit market via interest-rate changes themselves is very sluggish. The market, if disturbed from equilibrium and then left alone, would be only a quarter of the way back to equilibrium in a year. If the effectiveness of monetary policy depended on manipulating the rate of interest at which banks lend, it would be very slow indeed. (By the way, those who argue that interest rates have no effect at all on the demand for credit must explain why interest rates don't rise much further when credit is tight.) This may be the case. Or else it may be that both the apparent slowness and the weakness of the relation are explained by the fact that changes in supply and demand for credit work themselves out largely by changes in the stringency of *non-price* rationing of credit. It is not unknown in imperfect markets for the money price to be the most sticky of the many terms on which transactions take place. Changes in availability may be very fast; and they may carry a variable share of the adjustment at different times. Anyone who can develop a quarterly numerical measure of the degree of credit rationing from the supply side might be able to make real progress in this problem. (But do not fall into the trap of looking at the "quality" of successful borrowers *ex post*; that depends as much on the supply of high quality borrowers as on the standards imposed by banks. Everyone's balance sheet may improve in a boom.)

Inventory investment seems generally to be thought of as insensitive to interest rates and other credit conditions, despite the fact that the classical function of short-term bank lending to business is the provision of working capital. We have experimented with one model of inventory investment which does happen to yield a small but significant interest elasticity. It is hard to know how seriously to take this result; though the model in question is reasonable, it is only one out of several we tried, and not all of those gave such clear-cut results. We think this subject deserves further investigation, with special emphasis on the consequences of minor shifts in timing. The particular equation in question yields the prediction that a unit change in the interest rate or short-term bank loans (say from 5 percent to 4 percent, maintained forever) will ultimately stimulate between $4 and $5 billion worth of inventory investment. This is once and for all, not a continuing rate of investment. Just short of one quarter of this added inventory will be accumulated within three months of the change in interest rates; a bit over 40 percent will have been accumulated after six months; and just short of two-thirds will have taken place by the end of the year. This suggests a role for monetary policy in the short cycle. There is, however, a problem: as noted earlier, the bank lending rate appears to move sluggishly (availability effects may be quicker; if only there were some way of knowing). Our results suggest that if anything is to be done by the monetary authorities in the short run, they may have to be prepared to enforce larger swings in interest rates quickly. They have not done this in the postwar period. Also whatever the true state of affairs with respect to credit rationing may be, if our success in finding an interest-elasticity means anything perhaps it says something in favor of Tobin's proposal to have the Federal Reserve pay the discount rate on excess reserves and to permit commercial banks to pay interest on demand deposits. This would give the Federal Reserve firmer and quicker control over bank lending rates.

Turning now to fixed capital, we have found evidence that investment in equipment (measured by new orders for nonelectrical machinery) is somewhat sensitive to long-term interest rates. The implied elasticity is about −.4. But there is little doubt that monetary policy cannot count on having short-run stabilizing effects via fixed investment. Here the lag is undoubtedly very long, and for three reasons: (1) industrial bond yields and other long rates respond to monetary policy with a lag (the length of which we have not determined); (2) new orders respond to interest rates with a distributed lag (about which we are very insecure; but there is some evidence that a bit under half of the ultimate effect occurs in the first quarter after a change in interest rates, another 25 percent in the following quarter, and altogether about 90 percent in the course of a year; these figures need much further study); (3) and in a way most important, we have found that actual output in the capital goods producing sector responds quite sluggishly to new orders. Output of business equipment is well represented as a moving average of past new orders. It is clear from inspection that the production series fluctuates less than new orders, with the slack taken up by increasing backlogs when orders are high and decreasing backlogs when recession sets in. Some indication of the sluggishness with which a change in new orders makes itself felt in production is this: of the full long-run effect on production of a sustained increase in new orders, only about a seventh is felt in the first quarter after the increase and only about a half has been felt by the end of a year. On the assumption that at least the main effect of interest rate changes or other monetary policy actions is on new orders (rather than cancellations, for instance) this last lag alone is quite a substantial obstacle to effective short-run stabilization. Combined with the other two sources of delay it suggests that plant and equipment investment, while probably ultimately responsive to monetary policy, changes too slowly to be of use for countercyclical policy of the postwar variety.

Unfortunately we did not have time to do an analogous study of residential construction. Monetary policy appears to have been especially successful here during the postwar period, presumably because of the legislative ceilings on mortgage rates on VA loans. The precise timing remains to be studied.

But we can note here one bit of evidence — taken from VA and FHA records — which suggests that there is, on the average, a lag of approximately 3.5 months between the decision to build a house and the beginning of construction. ("Decision to build" is equated with the request for mortgage insurance, and "beginning of construction" is equated with the first compliance inspection.) Depending on how builders' orders and production of housing materials are related, this could be an overestimate. Also, there is no doubt a lag — still to be determined — between Federal Reserve action and changes in building plans, so this 3.5 month estimate should probably be taken as a minimum lag, considerably smaller than the total lag between Federal Reserve action and actual spending. (Seemingly, Richard Muth suggests as much in his study, "Demand for Non-Farm Housing," in Harberger, ed., *The Demand for Durable Goods*.) . . .

A Critique of Professor Friedman's Findings

This section is largely a report of our own attempt to estimate the outside lag of classical monetary policy, which loosely speaking is the lapse of time between the date on which the Federal Reserve takes action and the date on which the effects of this action on output and employment are realized. We begin, however, with a critique of Professor Friedman's much publicized work on the outside lag.[1]

His findings are nothing if not startling:

The rate of change of the money supply shows well-marked cycles that match closely those in economic activity in general and precede the latter by a long interval. On the average, the rate of change of the money supply has reached its peak nearly 16 months before the peak in general business and has reached its trough over . . . 12 months before the trough in general business . . . Moreover, the timing varies considerably from cycle to cycle — since 1907 the shortest time span by which the money peak preceded the business cycle peak was 13 months, the longest 24 months; the corresponding range at troughs is 5 months to 21 months.[2]

And both of Professor Friedman's assertions about the outside lag — that it is of considerable length, and that it is highly variable — have significance for the practice of monetary policy. Even if the lead of monetary action over business conditions were regular, its sheer length would pose a difficult problem. Monetary contraction, initiated while the contemporary situation clearly called for it, might have its effects at a time when its consequences would be perverse, in terms of the then ruling state of affairs. It would take an unrealistically good capacity to forecast on the part of the monetary authorities to conduct an accurate stabilization policy under these circumstances. But even if forecasting ability should improve, the fact that the length of the lag may itself vary unpredictably by as much as a year would place any conscious stabilization policy in danger of contributing to the instability it seeks to avoid.

[1] The research of Professor Thomas Mayer, reported in his "The Inflexibility of Monetary Policy" (*Review of Economics and Statistics,* November 1958), is not considered here, but only because we lacked sufficient time. For the same reason, the work of Dr. Clark Warburton, which is summarized in a series of papers published during the postwar period, is similarly ignored.

[2] "The Supply of Money and Changes in Prices and Output," in *The Relationship of Prices to Economic Stability and Growth,* Compendium of Papers Submitted by Panelists Appearing before the Joint Economic Committee (Washington, 1958), pp. 249–50. This reference does not give supporting detail, but such can be found in a paper by Beryl W. Sprinkel, "Monetary Growth as a Cyclical Predictor." *Journal of Finance* (September 1959), pp. 333–46.

For these reasons then, Friedman and others have advocated that the Federal Reserve abandon deliberate countercyclical policy and go over instead to a policy of causing the supply of money to increase regularly at some foreordained rate. This recommendation seems to assume tacitly that the Federal Reserve has essentially instantaneous control over the stock of money, which is at least open to doubt, especially in view of the history of the first half of 1960. However that may be, the basic empirical conclusion is clearly of fundamental importance for monetary policy, and we must therefore examine it critically.

(1) It is our view that Friedman's position is both empirically and logically untenable. That is to say, we claim two things. First: even given his general mode of approach, the data do not support the conclusion Friedman draws from them. Second: whatever the data say, the general mode of approach used by Friedman simply cannot bear the kind of interpretation he has placed on the results. There are yet other grounds on which one might reasonably object to (or at least desire to qualify) Friedman's methods and results. We will mention them later as possible hints for future research, but we have not pursued them.

(2) We take up the logical point first. Its significance extends beyond the question of the lag pattern in monetary policy, since Friedman has used the length and reliability of his lag as strong evidence that in the mutual interaction between the monetary sphere and the level of economic activity the causal thrust is primarily from the former to the latter.[3] Stripped to bare essentials, the Friedman-Sprinkel method is simply to plot a time series of some measure of the rate of change of the seasonally corrected stock of money.[4] If this series is compared with the National Bureau reference dates for general cyclical peaks and troughs, it is found that with great uniformity the peaks and troughs of the cycles in the monetary change series precede the business cycle peaks and troughs in the manner described. Since (to what degree of approximation?) the stock of money and its rate of change are what the monetary authorities wish them to be, we may identify the cause to be the peak or trough in monetary changes and the long-delayed effect to be the corresponding peak or trough in business activity.

---

[3] "The Supply of Money and Changes in Prices and Output," *op. cit.*, p. 251.

[4] It does not matter much at what point in the chain of decreasingly liquid near-moneys the line is drawn.

The unreliability in this line of argument is suggested by the following *reductio ad absurdum*. Imagine an economy buffeted by all kinds of cyclical forces, endogenous and exogenous. Suppose that by heroic and perhaps even cyclical variation in the money supply and its rate of change, the Federal Reserve manages deftly to counter all disturbing impulses and to stabilize the level of economic activity absolutely. Then an observer following the Friedman method would see peaks and troughs in monetary change accompanied by a steady level of aggregate activity. He would presumably conclude that monetary policy has no effects at all, which would be precisely the opposite of the truth.

This hypothetical example illustrates by an extreme case an important truth. One cannot deduce conclusions about the effects of monetary policy or about their timing without making some hypothesis, explicit or implicit, about what the course of events would have been had the monetary authorities acted differently. Such conclusions are *ceteris paribus* statements, partial derivatives, not total derivatives. There are rare occasions, cases of almost experimental control of extraneous factors, when it is safe (or at least irresistible) to make conclusions like this from a simple *ex post* record. But this is surely not one of those cases; there is no control of possible disturbances, and there is a long history of professional argument over the very point at issue. The Friedman argument is just about as sound logically as the claim that because interest rates tend to fall in recessions and private domestic investment does likewise, investment demand is necessarily positively related to interest rates.

We conclude therefore that as a matter of logic, the Friedman method cannot be interpreted as it has been. The observed pattern of peaks and troughs in the general business cycle and in the money supply and its increments is compatible with many hypotheses about why events turned out just so. For all we know, the cyclical peak occurring 16 months after a peak in the monetary series may have been fended off by monetary policy action for a year or more. There is no evading the necessity of beginning with some kind of model which permits one, for better or worse, to estimate the *ceteris paribus* effects of monetary policy.

(3) But suppose we waive the methodological point and look at the empirical analysis itself. A question which must have occurred to many students immediately arises: why choose the *rate of change* of the money supply as the measured indicator of monetary policy, rather than the stock of money itself? The possibility must be considered that this choice stacks the cards in favor of a long monetary

lead. Suppose that, apart from trends, the money supply and the level of activity move roughly simultaneously and that together they trace out fluctuations not too different from ordinary trigonometric oscillations. Then, as everyone knows, the rate of change in the stock of money will show an approximate quarter-cycle lead over business activity. And this is roughly what happens. The complaint can be made that this is an unnatural procedure, and that the equally unnatural procedure of plotting the rate of change of over-all activity against the stock of money would turn the lead into an equally long and erratic lag.

Against this criticism, Friedman has two replies, one based on expediency, the other on principle. The first is that the stock of money itself tends, because of its strong trend, to increase pretty much without interruption, business cycles showing themselves in a decreased rate of growth rather than in an absolute decline. If the data are to be analyzed by comparison at turning points, then obviously a monotonic series is useless, and it is natural to replace it by its rate of growth which does show well-marked cycles.

Secondly, this reply is reinforced by another consideration. A general belief that monetary factors influence aggregate activity does not entail any automatic conclusion as to whether the money stock, or its rate of change, or even some other characteristic, may be the natural time series to compare with the general state of business. So the changes in the money supply may well be the "right" series to use, and not merely the first difference of a more appropriate series.

Our own view is that only a play on words gets us into this purely verbal snare. From the policy point of view it is clearly immaterial whether we think in terms of M or changes in M. An agency which determines changes in M also determines M (except for an initial condition) and an agency which controls M also controls its rate of change. But it is not true, except in some irrelevant long-run sense, to say that the Federal Reserve controls either M or its rate of change. What the Federal Reserve can do is buy and sell in the open market, set reserve requirements, and set the discount rate. A little less directly, . . . we may say that the authorities control the effective primary reserves of the commercial banks (or at least the part of them which does not arise at the discount window); and at one further remove we may say that the measure of monetary policy is the power of the banking system to carry earning assets. This is what the monetary authorities *do;* they do not move a pointer on a dial marked M or even ΔM. The appropriate lag, significant both for policy and for analytical purposes, seems to us to be that between particular *actions* of the monetary authorities and the consequent events in the economy at large.

(4) But suppose we waive this point too, and agree to study the relations between M and/or ΔM and aggregate activity. How can we get around the absence of turning points in M, and somehow test the hypothesis that the lead of ΔM over general business is a mere reflection of an essentially simultaneous movement of M and general business? The simple observation seems never to have been made that instead of comparing the level of M and the level of economic activity we can compare the change in M with *the change* in economic activity. We have done this. . . . In summary [our results] overwhelmingly support the conclusion that the money supply itself and the level of aggregate output move more or less simultaneously over the business cycle, and that the lead of ΔM over aggregate output is a pure arithmetic artifact. From the observation of the last 40 years absolutely nothing can be inferred *by this method* about the causal interaction between the monetary sphere and the "real" sphere. . . .

The conclusion seems inevitable to us that the supply of money and the level of economic activity move approximately simultaneously. The most that we can squeeze out by way of a lead for the money supply is three months. The indubitable lead of the change in the money supply over the level of output follows arithmetically from this and has no causal significance at all. We must stress that it will not do to say, like a latter-day Galileo: "But nevertheless ΔM leads Q." True enough, it does. But so does ΔQ lead Q, [which] we have . . . shown. And it is no doubt equally true that ΔQ leads M. None of this can possibly offer any firm evidence about the web of cause and effect relationships connecting the real and monetary aspects of economic events, nor can it offer any *ex ante* guide to monetary policy.

CONCLUSION

The readings in this volume have included a variety of points of view on the effectiveness of monetary policy as a stabilizing tool and on the various, and sometimes conflicting, goals that must be considered. In recent decades economists have reached a broader consensus on the effectiveness of fiscal policy compared with monetary policy. In spite of the fact that monetary policy has enjoyed something of a comeback in favor in the last ten or fifteen years from its low status in the 1930's and '40's, for various reasons it still has a large number of detractors. On one hand is the Friedman view that it is a powerful instrument but that, when given discretionary power, even the wisest monetary authorities are likely to do more harm than good to the economy. On the other hand is the view of those who, following the kind of argument presented by Henderson in this collection of readings, question how important interest rates really are for investment decisions. Others, like Warren L. Smith, question the effectiveness of monetary policy on the grounds that central bankers have lost control because of the problems of a large public debt and the rise of financial intermediaries.

There are, at the same time, a number of students of monetary policy who, while not seeing it as the panacea envisaged by some economists in the 1920's, nevertheless look to discretionary policy as a significant and useful tool for stabilization purposes. In these readings, this general view is expressed by Rosa, Ascheim, Lerner, and Kareken and Solow. All these authors are certainly cognizant of the difficulties and complexities facing monetary authorities. And they would certainly all agree that other tools, especially fiscal policy ones, should be used. But even if prime emphasis is given to fiscal policy, the sense of these authors is that monetary policy ought to be used as a complementary tool in achieving the desired goals. This latter view represents the dominant thinking among economists today, but these readings should serve to demonstrate that there is a substantial and respected group of economists who disagree.

SUGGESTIONS FOR READING

The pioneering formulation of the role to be played by a central bank is contained in Walter Bagehot, *Lombard Street, A Description of the Money Market* (New York, Scribner, 1909).

A broad general statement outlining the goals and policies of modern central banks can be found in: Board of Governors of the Federal Reserve System, *The Federal Reserve System: Purposes and Functions* (Washington, 1963).

Two recent comprehensive studies of monetary institutions and policies undertaken in the United States and England are: The Report of the Commission on Money and Credit, *Money and Credit: Their Influence on Jobs, Prices and Growth* (Englewood Cliffs, N. J., 1961) and Great Britain Committee on the Working of the Monetary System (Chairman, the Rt. Hon. The Lord Radcliffe, G.B.E.) *Report* (London, 1959). The Radcliffe report is the less optimistic of the two with respect to the stabilization powers of monetary policy and this is due, in part, to the greater weight it attributes to the conflict of goals facing monetary authorities.

A detailed account of American monetary history is provided by M. Friedman and A. J. Schwartz in *A Monetary History of the United States, 1867–1960* (Princeton, 1963).

Earlier studies, undertaken in both England and the United States, and based on questionnaires to businessmen, concluded that changes in interest rates are unimportant in affecting investment decisions. See J. E. Meade and P. W. S. Andrews, "Summary of Replies to Questions on the Effects of Interest Rates," *Oxford Economic Papers,* No. 1 (Oct. 1938), and P. W. S. Andrews, "A Further Inquiry Into the Effects of Rates of Interest," *Oxford Economic Papers,* No. 3 (Feb. 1940). The above two articles are reprinted in *Oxford Studies in the Price Mechanism,* T. Wilson and P. W. S. Andrews, eds. (Oxford, 1951) pp. 27–30, 51–67. J. F. Ebersole, "The Influence of Interest Rates Upon Entrepreneurial Decisions in Business — A Case Study," *Harvard Business Review* (Autumn, 1938), XVII, pp. 35–40. For a criticism of these and other

129

similar studies, see William H. White, "Interest Inelasticity of Investment Demand – The Case From Business Attitude Surveys Reexamined," *American Economic Review* (Sept. 1956), XLVI, pp. 565–587.

The view that the rise in importance of financial intermediaries has reduced the effectiveness of monetary policy can be found in J. G. Gurley and E. S. Shaw, "Financial Aspects of Economic Development," *American Economic Review* (Sept. 1955), XLV, pp. 515–538. For a criticism of this thesis, see J. M. Culbertson, "Intermediaries and Monetary Theory: A Criticism of the Gurley-Shaw Theory," *American Economic Review* (March, 1958), XLVIII, pp. 119–131. An interesting commentary on this theme, from a somewhat different perspective, is contained in H. P. Minsky's "Central Banking and Money Market Changes," *Quarterly Journal of Economics*, Vol. LXXI, No. 2 (May 1957), pp. 171–187.

A classic study in favor of rules over discretion in monetary policy is that by Henry Simons in his "Rules Versus Authorities in Monetary Policy," *Journal of Political Economy* (Feb. 1936), XLIV, pp. 1–30; reprinted in H. C. Simons, *Economic Policy in a Free Society* (Chicago, 1948), pp. 160–183. For support of this view and paralleling Friedman's proposal calling for a constant increase in the money supply, see Edward S. Shaw, "Money Supply and Stable Economic Growth," *United States Monetary Policy*, Revised Edition, edited by Neil H. Jacoby (New York, 1964), pp. 73–93.

In addition to the selection in these readings, a fuller statement by Friedman, in support of his conclusion that monetary policy works only after a long lag, can be found in his "The Lag in Effect of Monetary Policy," *Journal of Political Economy* (Oct. 1961), LXIX, pp. 447–466. For another article in support of this view, see Thomas Mayer, "The Inflexibility of Monetary Policy," *Review of Economics and Statistics* (Nov. 1958), XL, pp. 358–374. Arguments disputing the existence of a long lag can be found in W. H. White, "The Flexibility of Anticyclical Monetary Policy," *Review of Economics and Statistics* (May 1961), LXIII, pp. 142–147, and in two articles by J. M. Culbertson, "Friedman on the Lag in Effect of Monetary Policy," *Journal of Political Economy* (Dec. 1960), LXVIII, pp. 617–621 and "The Lag in Effect of Monetary Policy: Reply," *Journal of Political Economy* (Oct. 1961), LXIX, pp. 467–477.

An article which defends the efficacy of monetary policy in the face of a wide range of criticisms is that by James R. Schlesinger, "Monetary Policy and Its Critics," *Journal of Political Economy* (Dec. 1960), LXVIII, pp. 601–616.